THROUGH THE WATCHES OF THE NIGHT

Spiritual reflections for medical students and residents

Through the Watches of the Night

Scott Conley M.D.

ISBN: 1977772560
ISBN-13: 978-1977772565

For Tracy, who has been with me
on this medical journey
since the beginning

Contents

Psalm 63:1-8

You, God, are my God,

    earnestly I seek you;

I thirst for you,

    my whole being longs for you,

    in a dry and parched land

    where there is no water.

I have seen you in the sanctuary

    and beheld your power and your glory.

Because your love is better than life,

    my lips will glorify you.

I will praise you as long as I live,

    and in your name I will lift up my hands.

I will be fully satisfied as with the richest of foods;

    with singing lips my mouth will praise you.

On my bed I remember you;

    I think of you **through the watches of the night.**

Because you are my help,

    I sing in the shadow of your wings.

I cling to you;

    your right hand upholds me.

Introduction

Medical school and residency comprise an unprecedented time in a person's life. During no other stage does such a focus of intense study and deluge of information meet such a rising burden of responsibility. And it so happens this period of training usually coincides with the formative years in a twenty-something's life, a critical time when the prefrontal cortex finally matures, and identity and values solidify. It's also when medical "habits" form—patterns and styles of approaching medicine and patient interactions that will last a career.

Add to this a student or resident of Christian faith, who desires to follow God and honor him with life and career. Let alone the challenges of getting a medical education and growing up at the same time; this Christian must also wrestle with integrating the newly-acquired education into the pursuit of Christlikeness. And believe me, there are many times these two seem worlds apart.

A fortunate Christian student or resident will secure a medical mentor: someone who has been there, who has wrestled with issues of faith and medicine and can come alongside to share this wisdom. Unfortunately, I fear these mentors are like rare diseases—they are infrequently encountered. The hectic pace and volume of responsibility in medicine see to it that many such potential mentors cannot afford the time to invest in the next generation.

That's where this book comes in. I wish I had something like it when I was in training. I didn't have a medical mentor, and I knew I was the worse without one. Having an experienced companion, at least in written form, to help me when I stood scratching my head at the intersection of faith and medicine would have been invaluable.

While there is no substitute for God's Word and the movement of the Holy Spirit in the lives of believers, I offer this short work simply as a collection of case studies from one who has been there. Not as someone who has reached perfection or expertise in any of this, but as someone still on the journey himself.

I envision this book as a devotional of sorts. I picture you taking fifteen minutes or so, perhaps when you are on call or during a break from your studies, to read a chapter. Each chapter stands alone, separate from the rest. Several themes repeat throughout the book, but similar chapters were purposefully separated. Use the questions at the end of each chapter to go deeper and apply the truths to your life. Don't neglect those application questions. Try them out, that very day or that week. One of my favorite quotes, mentioned in this book, is from A.W. Tozer: "Truth, to be understood, must be lived." Living out what we learn is the proof that we truly learned it.

I pray this book encourages you, challenges you, and helps you live out a growing faith during the epic adventure of medical training.

—Scott

One

Comparisons

I don't like exercise fanatics. You know the ones—those brady-cardics who don't stop working out even while on vacation. It's 90 degrees on a summer afternoon in Times Square and some guy from Ohio jogs past, weaving through the camera-wearing crowds. Or you're returning to your Orlando hotel at eight o'clock after stuffing yourself silly at dinner, when you walk past the fitness room and notice a fellow guest on the elliptical. *Can't they give it a rest?*

I must admit though, a good morning jog while vacationing at the beach atones for the dietary indiscretions of the night before. Besides, you can't beat the scenery: tumbling ocean waves drumming a soothing cadence on a sun-soaked morning; chipper seagulls squawking morning greetings; water-cooled breezes carrying a salty aroma; tide-washed beaches awaiting sunbathers eager to claim prime real estate for the day's solar absorption.

Morning jogs at the beach provide a refreshing change from my normal neighborhood circuit. They're also when my private exercise goes public. I have the opportunity to see how well I run compared to others. At home, I run alone and don't use a stopwatch. I don't sign up for 5K's or benefit races. I don't know if I am embarrassing myself or perhaps untapped Olympic material.

One morning jog on the boardwalk in Cape May, New Jersey had all the makings of a great run—perfect weather to enjoy, few crowds to navigate, no side stitches to endure—until something new happened to me: another runner raced by. Let it be known, I could have ignored someone who looks to be training for the Boston Marathon. But this guy looked like me—knee-length basketball shorts, sweat-stained cotton t-shirt, and measurable body fat. He had no right to be running faster than me. I tried to ignore him but my ego didn't approve of what happened. He had disrupted my aerobic bliss. A surge of competitive *Oh no you didn't!* welled up from within. As I circled around for my last lap on the boards, I concocted a plan to catch my passer—and beat him to the finish line of a race he didn't know he was now competing in.

Calling upon all the remaining energy from my breakfast of donuts and orange juice (that's carb loading, right?), I shifted into high gear. The sights and sounds of God's creation so glorious around me faded as I zeroed in on my opponent's sweaty back like an army sniper. My calculated pursuit paid off as the distance between us shrunk fast.

The music in my head, borrowed from *Chariots of Fire*, swelled with every inch the gap closed. Then, with heaving chest and flaming thighs, I caught him steps before the (imaginary) finish line. I held my breath as I passed him to conceal my respiratory struggle. Crossing the (again, imaginary) finish line first, I smiled in victory. Sure, it had taken every ATP molecule in my body to catch him, but I did it—I was the Eternal Boardwalk Master Runner of the Universe!

As I pulled up and leaned over to restore oxygen to my vital organs (just in time) and gloat in breathless victory, I noticed my opponent coming toward me—and right past me. He continued to run to the end of the boardwalk, down the exit ramp, and glide down the street until he was too far to see.

I wasn't in the mood for a victory lap anyway.

Just when we think we are on top of our game, someone comes along and makes us look like a novice. The moment I raise my arms in triumph as King of the Hill, I am knocked off my perch. You ace the anatomy test and are flying high, feeling good about your career choice; the next one you bomb (while your friend gets an A), and you wonder if you should have listened to your mother and become a lawyer. One day you nail the answer when pimped by an attending; the next you can't even think of a good guess to his question and feel like a fool when another resident answers with ease.

And so goes our opinion of ourselves, rising and falling between crests of pride and shallows of despair. Our emotions yo-yo with every victory and every failure, dragging along our self-confidence on a wild and unpredictable ride. And yet there is no getting around the fact that comparison is an integral part of our training in each phase. How else can you know where you rank in your college, medical school, or residency class but by sizing yourself up to your classmates? How else can you know if you will make a good doctor? Perhaps I make a good diagnosis, but what if my classmates have made a dozen more? I need to know where I stand!

> We do not dare to classify or compare ourselves with some who commend themselves. When they measure themselves by themselves and compare themselves with themselves, they are not wise.... But, "Let the one who boasts boast in the Lord." For it is not the one who commends himself who is approved, but the one whom the Lord commends.
>
> 2 Corinthians 10:12-13, 17-18

If a fool builds his house upon the sand, as the old children's song goes, then comparing ourselves to others is like laying footers across the beach. We'd fire that builder in a heartbeat. And yet we think nothing of constructing our identities on a foundation that hinges on performance and opinion. The practice of medicine is hard enough; why do we put ourselves through this torture and stupidity?

The Apostle Paul, the author of 2 Corinthians, is being kind when he says comparison is not wise in the passage above. The act of comparison is not just foolish; it's a two-edged sin. I sting from the burn of envy as I come up short in light of others' achievements, and I battle the rip current of pride when I grow smug in my successes.

Brennan Manning writes in *The Ragamuffin Gospel*, "We fluctuate between castigating ourselves and congratulating ourselves because we are deluded into thinking we save ourselves." Similarly, we toggle between the same two states in medicine because we are deluded into thinking we are solely responsible for our careers.

There is a better way. Growth as a Christian physician requires you to realize God's presence in your career. Hear me out before you claim this as obvious. The choice to become a doctor was not ultimately yours; God preordained it from the beginning. What God announced to Jeremiah at the start of his career, he declares to you: "Before I formed you in the womb I knew you, before you were born I set you apart; I appointed you" (Jeremiah 1:5). He created you for and called you to medicine. And then he didn't simply drop you off at your medical school front door with a pat on the shoulder, driving off to watch your life unfold from his rearview mirror.

He is with you in the lecture hall, the exam room, or the operating suite, carefully sculpting your career with his divine hands.

Every medical fact learned, every patient encountered, and every diagnosis made is a provision from his hands. It's his initiative. It's his power at work in your life. It's his promise to see it through to completion. In her devotional, *He Restores My Soul,* Jennifer Kennedy Dean notes, "Everything that God requires *of you*, he has already provided *for you.*"

This is no shallow puddle of provision. His resources are more vast than the Atlantic, stretching beyond the horizons of minds, even our imaginations. No wonder Paul, as he considers God's presence and power at work in the lives of believers, cannot help but end his prayer for the Ephesians with effusive praise: "Now to him who is able to do immeasurably more than all we ask or imagine, according to his power that is at work within us, to him be glory in the church and in Christ Jesus throughout all generations, for ever and ever!" (Ephesians 3:20).

This does not absolve you from any role in your career, any less striving. Rather, it should take the pressure off. Now you don't have to struggle to wade through medical school or residency while at the same time laboring to construct your identity out of the fragile materials of performance and opinion. Freedom is found when we put down the plastic buckets and stop our frantic attempts to repair the crumbling castle we think somehow defines us.

Absent within this freedom is any tendency toward comparing ourselves to others. We no longer have any need for this measuring stick, which turns out to be too short anyway. Besides, basing your competence and confidence on how you measure up to others will fail, giving way beneath your feet like sand. Resting in God's calling and provision and ongoing presence in your career is stable terrain.

Building your career on this foundation not only allows you to face the storms that will blow through your life, but also to withstand the relentless tides and tenacious currents of 21st century medicine.

I won't be challenging anyone to a foot race again anytime soon. The competition I created that day ruined an otherwise enjoyable morning jog. I find greater and lasting satisfaction when I focus on my exercise for its true purposes and stop looking around for external measures of my competence. Only then can I find joy in the journey. The same can be said for doctoring.

Questions for reflection

1. Think of a recent example when you compared yourself to others. Describe it below. What was the result? Did you feel better or worse about yourself?

2. How do you view God's involvement in your medical career so far?

_____Watching in his rearview mirror as he drives away?

_____Sitting on his courtroom bench judging your every move?

_____Shaking his head in disappointment at your failures?

_____Writing the next chapter as you seek to follow his movement in your life?

How does your answer line up with what the Bible says about God?

3. What is one way this week you can transfer your confidence and competence off the shaky ground of comparison and onto the firm foundation of God's love for you?

Two

Call me maybe

More fear than my first time driving on a highway, my first day of medical school, and my wedding day—combined.

It was my first intern night on call.

The ink was still drying on my medical school diploma. Was it legal to be a doctor at twenty-seven years old? I wasn't ready for this. As hard as I tried, I couldn't conjure up a single medical fact to calm my panic-stricken brain. Suddenly medical school didn't seem so bad after all. I wanted to run back to the comfort of my short coat and hide behind my textbooks.

I still remember the first time the little black beeper went off that night. Forget adenosine—I'm sure I went asystolic for a few seconds. *Wait, the ICU? My first page is from the ICU? What could I possibly know that those ICU nurses didn't? Why couldn't the first call have come from a cafeteria worker looking for some nutrition advice?* I swallowed hard, went out through the residency lounge door, and into my career.

Thankfully, I survived that night and gained confidence with each call that came and went. It wasn't long however, being on Q3 call, until I began to dread those shifts. The anxiety of the first call night was quickly replaced by annoyance. What was the point of this scheduled insomnia? How much could I possibly learn at 3:00 a.m.? The nights became an endless stream of chest pain, shortness of breath, falls out of bed, fevers, inconsolable children, and constipation. My goal with each patient was to tuck them in and get back to bed myself.

Then one night, God changed the way I looked at call. Though I was deep into my third year and had managed a variety of cases, I had yet to care for a patient with shock. I worried that I would graduate soon and not be able to recognize or manage shock out in the real world.

The page woke me from a rare sleep. "Low blood pressure" flashed on the tiny beeper screen, the call back number belonging to the cardiac telemetry floor. After taking a minute to allow my brain to boot up, I called the floor.

"We have a patient who was admitted for chest pain but now his blood pressure is dropping fast. You'd better get up here."

Skipping the elevator and sprinting up five flights of stairs helped wake me up. As I entered the room, I encountered a semiconscious man in his seventies, lying flat with legs elevated, surrounded by an entourage of nurses wrestling with large bore IVs. The facts returned quickly as I fired off questions to the staff. After a targeted exam, I realized I was dealing with a man in shock. Without knowing it, I had already ticked through several possible causes in my mind. Stat labs confirmed my suspicion—septic shock. I woke the attending cardiologist, ran the case past him, and transferred the patient to the ICU.

Was I bound to encounter a patient in shock during my training? Probably. Does God always assuage my fears in such a well-timed manner? No, but he sure did that night. While teaching me what septic shock looked like, God also showed me that call is not just a random string of events I stumble into bleary-eyed each evening. They are experiences that he, the Creator of the Universe, has handcrafted and prepared for me. Not that I dismiss random events occurring in this world; they're just random this side of heaven. And while God designs my call nights to sharpen and expand my medical knowledge, his purposes in them are much bigger.

Through the watches of the night, God challenges me, encourages me, grows me. He provides me chances to show love when I don't feel like it. He pushes me all night to teach me perseverance. He stretches me to the end of myself so I learn dependence on him. He opens my eyes to see each patient encounter as a divine appointment scheduled by him. Call is not simply a training ground for my medical career; it is also a mold in which God forms me into Christlikeness. When I began to look at call this way, it became more palatable. I hunted for God's fingerprints in my night watches in the hospital, and you know, I found them.

Do you believe this? Do you believe God is in your call? Paul writes in Romans 8:28, "In all things God works for the good of those who love him." Why wouldn't this include those late nights in the hospital? Searching for his divine activity in your call is not only encouraging, it bestows a deep and transcendent purpose on the experiences. It gives meaning and significance to the randomness. And even better, God promises success when we search for him. God says in Jeremiah 29, "You will seek me and find me when you seek me with all your heart."

Even at 3:00 a.m.

Questions for reflection

1. What has been the scariest moment in your medical training so far? Looking back, how did you see God at work in the situation?

2. What obstacles prevent you from seeking God with all your heart in these moments?

3. In what situation or task this week can you look for God's fingerprints?

Three

The thrill of victory

Courageous. Passionate. Poetic. David was a central figure in the Old Testament and in the history of Israel. The Bible is full of stories from his early years and reign as king. And while scripture does not hold back in detailing his alarming sins and failures, when David got it right, boy, he got it right! The lessons we can mine from his successes are rich indeed.

1 Chronicles 11 tells one such story. In the opening scene of the chapter, the once-anonymous shepherd boy is crowned King of Israel. The next scene details King David and his army capturing the impenetrable fortress known as Jerusalem from the Jebusites. The Israelites nickname the city after David. The new king quickly grows more and more powerful with each God-given victory. David's army is strong, led by a bunch of mega-studs known as the Thirty—mighty warriors who would make the Avengers look like a bunch of third-graders. Life couldn't get any better for David.

Except . . . he could use a glass of water.

David meets up with some of the Thirty at the cave of Adullam, most likely to scope out the enemy Philistine army that has amassed nearby. It must have burned David up that part of the Philistine army occupied his hometown of Bethlehem. Perhaps that got him reminiscing about his earlier years as some of the Thirty over-hear David longing for a drink of water from his favorite hometown watering hole.

"Oh, that someone would get me a drink of water from the well near the gate of Bethlehem!" (verse 17). I'm sure David didn't mean for anyone to actually do it. But three of the Thirty hear his longing and hatch a hare-brained plan to get the water for him. So they bust through the enemy lines, outnumbered the entire time, to fetch a pail of water. Sounds like a testosterone-laden nursery rhyme!

I bet the Three couldn't suppress their huge smiles as they saun-tered up to David and said, "We have a gift for you, our King!" How could David not have been flabbergasted when he saw the water and learned where it was from?

Truth be told, scripture reports David was not happy with his mighty warriors for risking their lives like a bunch of frat brothers with no brain cells. He refused to drink the water because of the risk they took.

But imagine what David *could* have done with the water. David could have poured himself a glass of Bethlehem's Finest, raised it high, offering a toast to his heroic Thirty and to his own Kingly Greatness. He could have used the cool water as high-octane fuel for his own royal hubris. And who would have blamed him? The nation of Israel is entering its heyday and the handsome young king is at the head of the pack. He's got a cold one in his right hand and the remote control of his destiny in the other. Life is good. Real good.

But what does David do instead? He pours the drink on the ground. David gives the water a greater meaning and purpose than just satisfying his thirst at that moment. David passes on this pleasure and potential symbol of power, turning it instead into a sign of humble devotion to God. The Bible says David, "poured it out to the Lord" (verse 18). He denies himself the glory knowing only God deserves that much. David is acutely aware God was the one who hand-picked him out of the fields to be king. It's God who supplies his victories. It's God alone who deserves the credit. And so, in front of his warriors, David worships the True King by making a puddle at his feet.

No doubt on this one—David is a man after God's own heart.

So, a question surfaces: When we score a victory, when we nail a diagnosis, when everything is going our way, who gets the credit? Adversity can bring out the best in a person, but how I handle victories is just as instructive and telling about my character.

Remember the page from the ICU during my first call night as an intern? I was summoned to see a woman who had been admitted for unstable angina. When I arrived at the bedside, the nurse introduced me to a pale woman who was vertiginous and vomiting profusely. While performing a way-too detailed exam as only an intern would do, I discovered the patient had a grossly abnormal finger-to-nose test on her left side. Between wretches I had her repeat the test several times to be sure. I was astounded that the neurological exam actually worked! I concluded the patient was not suffering from a heart problem but rather likely from an occipital infarct.

Unfortunately, the ICU attending did not share my excitement when I called to relay my discovery. He knew I was an intern and knew the date was July 2nd. The morning team would see the patient in a few hours and take of her, he stated coldly; he then hung up on me. Yet I just knew it was an infarct. The patient needed a stat MRI, but I didn't have the guts that night to supersede the attending and order it. Heck, I didn't even know what dose of IV promethazine to give her to stop the vomiting—the nurse told me what to order. So how could I be so bold as to think that I, a super-green intern, knew of a diagnosis others much more seasoned had missed?

You can guess what the ICU team ordered later that morning after reading my passionate on-call note. The stat brain MRI proved I was right. Thankfully, the patient recovered well. But that victory was a huge confidence booster to a scared young man who had been a doctor for a grand total of forty-nine hours. I knew then that I would make it in this profession.

And yet, who deserves the praise for the victory?

When I diagnose an acute MI (with tombstones on the EKG) during my first week of practice in a patient who thought he simply had a cold, or pick up a case of acute rheumatic fever that others missed, or impress a father by diagnosing strep throat by looking at his son's feet (the boy had erythema nodosum), who gets the credit?

Do I raise a glass and toast myself for the great diagnoses and the fabulous saves I made? Or do I give credit where credit is due and realize only God deserves that much glory?

Giving God props actually makes me stronger because it places me in my proper position: one of grateful dependence on him. Hoarding the credit for myself as I gulp down the praise for my victory feels good for a while—until I realize my cup is then empty. And despite my repeated attempts, I can't keep it full. The victories become less and less powerful to fill my cup, and my mistakes and failures create leaks in the bottom. But when I follow David's example and give God the glory for my successes, when I give God the credit and rely on him for every diagnosis in every patient encounter, he offers free refills with his unlimited power.

I am not a Vulcan. I am a human with emotions that bubble to the surface in any situation, especially with victories. I am not saying we should pour out all the happiness or joy we might feel when we succeed. Stoicism is not the goal. What I am saying is, as Eugene Peterson notes, joy needs to come, "from feeling good not about yourself but about God." Like the credit for a victory, the joy from success needs to be properly assigned.

For David, the act of pouring out a symbol of his victories was an exercise in proper credit placement. We all need to practice a little glass-tipping with each victory that comes our way.

Questions for reflection

1. Think of a victory you have had already in your medical career—maybe acing a Biochem exam or Step 1 of the Boards, or making a great diagnosis on a patient. Looking back, what was your response? Did you toast a glass to yourself or pour it out to God?

2. How can you develop a joy that feels good about God rather than yourself?

Four

One breezy summer afternoon I was standing in front of a monkey cage at the Cape May Zoo. Built near the New Jersey shore, this zoo is a wonderful community park with over 250 species of animals in thoughtful displays and realistic habitats. But the best part about the place? Free admission! Where can you go for free these days?

While the monkeys were entertaining with their slap-stick routines and gymnastic feats that summer day, something else in their enclosure caught my attention. Scampering across the cage floor were several animals who obviously did not belong to the primate family. Sporting gray fur coats and stubby legs, these creatures looked like a bunch of pregnant squirrels minus the bushy tails. I figured they must be a type of rodent I had never seen before. The monkeys ignored them, but I couldn't help but wonder: *Why were they here, with the monkeys? Did these creatures belong in the cage, or did they break in on a daring raid to swipe bananas?*

I spotted a wall plaque near the cage that convinced me their presence was intended. The floor-skitterers were known as *rock hyrax*, a small land-based mammal found in parts of Africa and the Middle East. My first impression? Boring—at least compared to the monkeys. No tails for swinging, no comical facial expressions, no opposable thumbs. I stopped to watch the furry critters only because of their peculiar location in the zoo. Had a zookeeper been nearby, I would have asked why the rock hyrax weren't housed with other rodents. Why were they stuck with the primates? Did the zoo run out of space for them?

Turns out rock hyrax are not rodents, but rather in their own unique family, the wall plaque reported. But what the description said next stopped me in my tracks. Turns out the rock hyrax are the closest living relative to . . . the *elephant*. I had to read this a few times to make sure I had it right. The elephant? Really? How could this creature, whose name comes from the Greek for 'shrew mouse', be consanguineous with the largest land animal on the planet? Must be a hiccup in the zoological classification system, I figured. Perhaps a little zookeeper humor slipped in for fun.

I couldn't help but believe it was accurate. (Google later confirmed it to be true.) In that moment in the zoo, I experienced an immediate transformation of opinion. Instantly I viewed the rock hyrax in a new light because of this information. The closest relative to the elephant? That's crazy! This anonymous, squirrel-like, non-rodent became noteworthy to me, capturing my attention, simply because of its association with something greater.

Frances Schaeffer wrote, "Because a man is a man, he is to be loved at all cost."

What is a man? The result of a cosmic accident? A random collection of beneficial evolutionary mutations? Or the work of a Master Craftsman made in his image? Since life without meaning is such a drag, I am partial to believe the latter option. So, then it follows, because of this association with the Creator, each human life takes on extraordinary significance. Every person in this big human zoo, no matter how mundane or plain, anonymous or insignificant, ugly or disabled, emaciated or impoverished, has incredible intrinsic worth. Human value is not quantified from job title or skin color, not from social standing or even from accomplishments. Each person's worth comes from the fact that their closest living relative is God himself.

This is helpful to remember in the medical field. During our training, we are at great risk of unintentionally developing not only a finely-tuned hubris but also a thickly-calloused heart. The collision of the two makes us specialists at labeling and stereotyping those we meet with laser precision. Supreme Court justices have nothing on us as we judge from our lofty benches of opinion with brutal zeal.

Don't believe me? Take a moment to honestly fill in the blanks to the following statements:

Obese people are _____.
Medical Assistance patients are _____.
Smokers are _____.
Teen moms are _____.
Narcotic-dependent patients are _____.

What comes to mind with each of these statements? I am ashamed what leaps into mine. All the while, we miss the wall plaque on each patient's heart which reads, *Imago Dei*.

There is more here than just right thinking. It's about right *doing* as well. Take a recent example from my primary care practice: A prescription drug-addicted single mother reeking of cigarette smoke asks me (as I was heading out the exam door) to remove a skin tag from her neck at the end of her office visit. Do I roll my eyes in annoyance— especially since she has no medical insurance and I will not get paid for the procedure—or do I notice there's a few minutes to spare and show her some dignity by doing a quick snip? (Under sterile conditions, of course).

My prayer is that I grow in Christlikeness to the point where my thoughts about and actions toward every patient would honor their worth. And I pray that each time I look a patient in the eye, I will recall their connection to the Almighty God and remember the lesson learned from an unlikely elephant relative.

Questions for reflection

1. Which type of patient do you struggle to love the most?

2. Why do we tend to stereotype the people we meet?

3. 1 Samuel 16:7 says, "The Lord does not look at the things people look at. People look at the outward appearance, but the Lord looks at the heart." What can you do this week to see people for who they are?

Five

Moments around the fire

The warmth from the courtyard fire was inviting, but he dared not get too close. Finding a bench a safe distance from the fire, he adjusted the cloak, hiding his face as he sat. Despite an overwhelming need to see what was happening, he feared being recognized in the light of the fire. For a moment, a brief shiver shook his body. Were these chills from the coolness of the night air—or from nerves? Everything was happening so fast, so many thoughts racing in his head, so many things he didn't understand. . . .

Suddenly he felt the weight of eyes staring at him. His pulse quickened as he trained his gaze on a small rock at his feet. Eye contact would be bad. Immediately he regretted his decision to come here. Could he escape if recognized? Were soldiers nearby? If only he still had his sword.

From the direction of the staring came a female voice: "This man was with him!" Just the words he hoped not to hear. Unable to resist the urge, he glanced up and saw a young girl pointing at him. Others warming around the fire stopped talking and were staring too. His eyes grew big in fear. His tachycardia worsened. Peter wasn't chilly anymore.

This is Peter's *moment around the fire*. As flickering light from the courtyard flames reflected off his sweat-stained brow the night of Jesus' arrest, Peter faced a decision. How would this former fisherman turned disciple of Jesus respond to this accusation of association? Would he identify with Christ or distance himself from his friend and Lord? It's a decision he would have to make in an instant. There was no time to mull it over. No time to draw up a chart listing the pros and cons. No time to cast lots or ask the Magic 8 Ball app. And Peter couldn't walk away from this one, as walking away would be to choose. He had to decide.

This Good Friday story from Luke 22 is familiar. You know what Peter chose—denial. Not just once, but three times. He chose self-preservation over loyalty, safety over integrity. He chose to fit in rather than stand up. He chose backside-covering cowardice over God-insured courage. Strong and loyal Peter, willing to die for Jesus a few hours earlier, came up short when it counted most.

Peter immediately felt the consequences of his decision. The rooster crowed, reminding Peter of a somber prediction of betrayal. Luke reports that Jesus, who was being held nearby, "turned and looked straight at Peter" (verse 61). That look—filled not with anger and hatred but with a compassionate sadness—was enough to cause Peter's heart to explode with regret.

We all have moments around the fire, moments shaped by a decision. A crude joke is told at morning rounds. Someone speaks of another resident, a patient, or an attending in a disparaging way. Gossip spreads about a fellow med student. Belief in God is ridiculed. A patient asks you to fudge on his disability papers. What's your response? Will you stand up and show loyalty to Christ or distance yourself from him? In moments like these, you only have an instant to decide. Many times, you can't walk away. Do you stand up for what is right and true? Or does your laughter, your silence, or your response expose your denial? Too often, like Peter, I cave in a fit of self-preservation and throw Jesus under the bus to save my hide.

Peter was lucky. At least he was shown the error of his ways immediately. And while it caused him deep sorrow and bitter weeping, he could deal with his sin right away. Worse for me, there is no rooster crow or glance from Jesus to shock me back into reality when I choose poorly. Usually nothing happens. At least not that I can see. Conversations move on, the activities of the day continue unabated. So what's the big deal, you ask? There are worse sins to commit, aren't there? But deep within the damage has been done. A small callous forms over a segment of my heart. The next time around the fire it's a little easier to decide, a little easier to ignore the Spirit's warning prompts, a little easier to deny.

Maybe the moments we face don't seem as weighty as Peter's in the course of Christian history, but consider A.W. Tozer's thoughts:

> Our choices reveal what kind of persons we are, but there is another side to the coin. We may by our choices also determine what kind of persons we will become. We humans are not only in a state of being, we are in a state of becoming.

If it's true my life is shaped by the decisions I make, then the choices I make in those little moments around the fire are just as critical to shaping my character as the big decisions. Think about it: is it the rare flood that gives shape to a stone lodged in the creek bed, or is it the constant, unrelenting trickle of water over the rock that determines its form? The decisions I make today craft my character tomorrow.

A few hours later, Jesus would hang on a cross for his friend Peter, whose words of betrayal still echoed in the nearby courtyard.

Yet Jesus didn't stop there. He specializes in redemption too. During a post-resurrection beach conversation with Peter (detailed in John 21), Jesus refashioned Peter's denial into a blow torch and welded his mission onto Peter's heart.

Jesus continues in this specialty today: forgiving us, redeeming us, then repurposing our sin and poor choices ultimately for our growth and his kingdom purposes. Praise God that Jesus' blood spilled that Good Friday covers you and me when we face moments around the fire.

Questions for reflection

1. Can you recall a recent moment around the fire? What were you feeling? What did you choose? How did you feel afterward?

2. Think of a sin or poor choice in your life God redeemed and used to grow you. Write about the experience here and take a moment to reflect on God's redeeming work in your life.

Six

Rocky

The year was 1980. Pac-man was released in the United States. The Philadelphia Phillies won the World Series. Mount Saint Helens erupted. I was in fifth grade at Glenside Elementary just outside of Philadelphia. And Rocky was my classmate.

Actually, his name was Ricky, but most who knew him called him Rocky. Larger than life, with thick black hair, an unmistakable Philly accent, and a street-sense swagger, he deserved all the similarities to the movie character who by then had defeated Apollo Creed in his Rocky II triumph.

Rocky and I were in fifth grade together—and that is where the similarities ended. I was scrawny and prepubescent. Rocky had muscles. I'm sure he had a chest hair or two. He towered over the rest of us even though, looking back, I doubt he was especially tall. His tough-as-nails aura added a good six inches to his height.

That year I also found myself in the middle of a love triangle. A blonde-haired, cowboy-boot-wearing girl named Debbie liked me, and she made this well known by slipping a love note in my desk one day. I wasn't into girls at the time, so I found the whole thing weird and embarrassing. The problem was, another boy in my class named Gary liked Debbie, and he was none too happy that Debbie liked me. I don't recall how it started, but one day at recess that year Gary challenged me to a fight over Debbie. And while the origin of the elementary school title fight eludes me, what I do remember is fear. Gary was tough—not Rocky tough—but there was a wildness in his eyes, and he had the start of biceps too. Given the above description of my bodily proportions, I was definitely the underdog on the fight card. Even worse, I wasn't a fast runner.

And so here I was, standing face-to-face with Gary on the blacktop near the basketball court, about to enter my first fight, hoping it wasn't my last. All ten years of my short life flashed before my eyes. And yet in that moment, as the first punch (probably to my face) was seconds away, something inexplicable occurred.

Rocky stepped between us.

Glaring at Gary, Rocky uttered a heroic line: "You'll have to go through me first."

Hollywood couldn't have gotten the timing any better.

Over thirty years later, I am still not sure why Rocky came to my rescue. Call it an act of fifth-grade altruism. Perhaps Rocky was just looking for a chance to pummel Gary for an unrelated reason. Or (could it be?) maybe Rocky actually considered me his friend. Regardless of the reason, here was this mountain of a boy standing between me and my enemy. He was standing up *for me*. In an instant, the tides turned. Power shifted. Victory was inevitable. Gary backed away.

Rocky's simple act created two distinct reactions inside me at that moment. If Rocky would step in and be willing to fight for me, then I figured I must be worth something. My confidence grew; pride swelled within me. Yet it was a pride based not on my own abilities, but rather founded in what Rocky (the most important person in that moment) thought of me. It was a sense of deep worth.

In the shadow of Rocky's broad shoulders, I also found security. I didn't need to prove myself. I didn't need to worry about self-preservation. Rocky's actions that day gave me a freedom which allowed me to take risks. I could peer around those broad shoulders, stick out my tongue, and say to my challenger, "Oh yeah? Let's see what you're made of now!"

Jesus' death was his way of stepping between us and our enemy and saying, "You'll have to go through me first." And while Rocky's motive was uncertain, Jesus' was crystal clear (cue John 3:16). As Jesus breathed his last upon the cross, the tide turned. Power shifted. Victory was inevitable.

Those of us who believe in what Jesus did on the cross need to recall afresh how he stepped in for us that day, saving us from certain defeat. When we do, I pray that it creates in us the same reactions of worth and confidence I experienced on the day Rocky stepped in for me.

But we need to ask ourselves what effect his sacrifice has had on our lives. I mean, in a really practical way. Do I truly grasp my worth in the light of God's love? If so, then why do I look to my Board scores and correct diagnoses for my sense of worth and identity? Does the reality of the cross make me more confident in who I am through Christ? If so, then why do I make decisions along each step of my medical career out of fear? Do I sense a freedom in my life thanks to his sacrifice? If so, then how does that freedom show up in my conversations with patients and colleagues?

Questions for reflection:

1. How *should* Jesus' death on the cross impact your worth and confidence?

2. How do you go about transferring your worth and confidence to God?

3. Look back over your decisions and actions from the past week. How many were made out of fear? How would the situations have been different if you had chosen or acted out of the freedom gained from Jesus' sacrifice?

4. What would your conversations this week based in freedom sound like?

Seven

Pride comes before…

It was my third year of residency. I was on rotation in the emergency department.

And I was on a roll.

If there is such a thing as "being in the zone" in medicine, I had found it. All month my diagnoses were dead on. Like a seasoned veteran, I ordered the right tests with precision and efficiency. No obscure condition evaded my detection. My treatment plans were accurate and evidence-based. I presented cases with the eloquence of Lincoln. Even my sutures looked perfect. Attendings heaped on accolades. Specialists gushed over my clinical acumen. Nurses stood in awe of my precocious skill. And by the end of the month, one attending even let me call him by his first name. If dabbing had been invented by then, I would have been posing all day. I could do no wrong.

Grabbing the next available chart one day late in the rotation, I strode confidently into the room of a waiting patient. An elderly gentleman who had obviously suffered a massive stroke lay motionless and barely conscious on the gurney. He was alone in the quiet, glass-walled exam room. After performing a targeted physical (the history was unobtainable), I turned to the male nurse who had just entered the room behind me and barked, "Looks like another Gomer. Let's order a Gomer smear." (In case you are not familiar, a *Gomer Smear* is the term for a panel of tests and imaging studies one would order on a *Gomer*, an acronym for "Get Out of My ER"—a crude term for an elderly patient, often unresponsive or demented, who is dropped off by an ambulance crew.)

As I walked out of the room, I ran into one of the attendings and told him about the patient. "We have a Gomer in Room 2 with left-sided hemiparesis. I ordered a Gomer smear."

"I'm glad you went in quickly to see that patient in Room 2," the attending replied without looking up, "he is the grandfather of the nurse who was in the room with you."

My face flushed and my stomach flopped. I had just called the nurse's grandfather a Gomer to his face. Yikes. But this was more than just an embarrassing put-my-foot-in-my-mouth moment. In that instant, a veil lifted from my eyes. I saw what kind of physician I had become that month in the ED. How could I have become so calloused? Through my arrogance, fueled by success and a burning desire to impress the attendings, my compassion and humility had been replaced by nauseating levels of hubris. Patients were no longer fellow humans to be cared for but diagnoses to be lauded for. My goal was not to ease suffering but to treat 'em and street 'em with the best. I measured success not by my compassion and service to patients but by the praise of my attendings. My selfish ambition had blinded me. I desperately sought forgiveness.

I'm sure Jesus never called anyone a Gomer. I doubt he ever whispered a leper joke to his disciples or rolled his eyes in front of a blind man. His encounters with people recorded in the Gospels were filled with unconditional love and compassion. Despite an extraordinarily hectic schedule that could rival the busiest physician's, he took the time to minister to those he met. People left their encounters with him physically healed and spiritually encouraged. He gave no one a label, put no one in a box; he saw all as precious creations of his Father and treated them as such.

How did Jesus do this so well? Because life wasn't about him. Though he was the creator of the universe, Jesus didn't strive to be the center of it. He didn't need to be; he was secure in his identity. This was never more evident than in a scene recorded in John 13, when Jesus washed his disciples' feet. The gospel writer John reports, "Jesus knew that the Father had put all things under his power, and that he had come from God and was returning to God; so he got up from the meal, took off his outer clothing and wrapped a towel around his waist. After that, he poured water into a basin and began to wash his disciples' feet, drying them with the towel that was wrapped around him." Jesus knew who he was, where he was going, what he had to do, and how much his Father loved him—that's all he needed. And though aware he would suffer and die a torturous death a few hours later, Jesus showed his friends the full extent of his love by serving them with the humblest of acts.

Jesus' love poured out on the dirty feet of his disciples was proof of his security and identity in God. In contrast, the selfish pride I splattered around the ED that month was evidence of my insecurity and pathetic attempts at self-worship. Where Jesus found freedom to focus on others, I was chained to my pride, desperately manipulating patient encounters to be all about me. Had we been in the NBA, Jesus would have lead the league in assists; I would have shot nothing but air balls in my attempt to be the hero who made the game-winning basket.

A.W. Tozer's description of a meek man fits this situation and the life of Jesus well:

The meek man cares not at all who is greater than he, for he has long ago decided that the esteem of the world is not worth the effort. . . . He knows well that the world will never see him as God sees him and he has stopped caring.

Pride is one of the deadliest cancers to the soul. Symptoms can be subtle and are often ignored at first. By the time it's detected, pride has often widely metastasized. Its aggressiveness is exceeded only by the pain involved in its eradication. The surgery needed can be extensive. Thankfully, we have a Surgeon who is both kind and skilled at healing us.

Of all the diagnoses I made that month, I missed one—in my own heart. I could have avoided a lot of trouble with early detection.

Questions for reflection

1. How does pride blind a person?

2. Where have you seen pride show up in your medical career so far?

3. David prays in Psalm 19, "But who can discern their own errors? Forgive my hidden faults." David recognized there was sin in his life he didn't even know about. Take a moment to confess your hidden faults to God and ask him to bring them into the light of his grace and mercy so you and he can deal with them.

Eight

Right here

Laughter fills the air as the adults in my extended family sit around the dining room table catching up on life stories since our last gathering. Thanksgiving dinner has been cleared and the kids are scattered throughout my brother's house playing Hide-and-Go-Seek. Every so often one of them scampers by, looking for a new hiding spot.

After several rounds of the game in the converted rancher, novel hiding places are increasingly scarce. My daughter Megan appears at the table looking desperate.

"I can't find any more good hiding spots," she says with eyes darting, the seeker's countdown audible from a distant room. Her time is dwindling fast.

Just then my brother says, "Megan, sit right here," as he points to an empty chair at the table between him and my dad. Megan gives him a quizzical look, not knowing what he's up to.

"Trust me," he says with a smirk.

With no time or other options left, my daughter obediently complies. Sensing what could happen, the adults hastily restart conversations where they left off. My daughter has no choice but to sit and wait.

As if on cue several minutes later, my niece (the seeker) walks into the room. And as if scripted, she reports, "I can't find Megan. Do you know where she is hiding?"

None of the adults have a good poker face, but we did our best to hide the churning mix of astonishment and amusement welling up as we watched her scan the room looking for an answer. None of us dared even a glance at Megan and risk blowing her perfect cover.

"No, we don't know where she is," came our reply. "Are you sure you checked everywhere upstairs?"

The seeker turned and left, heading toward the stairs. As soon as she was out of earshot, the dining room erupted.

If you are near a computer or reading this on an electronic device, Google the phrase "selective attention test." Watch the first YouTube video that appears in the search results from Daniel Simons and Christopher Chabris. Unless you have seen the video before, don't read any further until you watch the whole video and follow the instructions.

———————————

Simons and Chabris, the Harvard researchers who developed this video for their research, found almost half of viewers did not see the gorilla. I showed my dad the video while writing this. He didn't see the gorilla either.

The phenomenon is called *inattentional blindness*. Simons and Chabris' research reinforces the point that, "we perceive and remember only those objects and details that receive focused attention." Even when an object appears at the point of visual fixation, if attention is focused elsewhere and the object is unexpected, it may be missed. In other words, what you're not looking for, you may not see. My niece didn't see Megan sitting among the adults because she was not expecting her to be there. My dad (and 50 percent of you) didn't see the gorilla because he wasn't looking for it.

This principle can be applied spiritually as well, and with it comes powerful implications. Since I was handed my license to practice medicine, I have always struggled with spotting God in my days. Integrating faith and medicine has never come easy. Sure, many times I've felt a prompting to share a word of encouragement or to pray with a patient, and I credit God with bringing elusive diagnoses to mind when I have been stuck. But these episodes have not been frequent enough. The majority of my work days—bursting with countless tasks, interruptions, and responsibilities—end up becoming exercises in inattentional blindness.

But what if God is right here in my office, walking around in a gorilla suit, and I've totally missed him? With my attention so focused on the nuances and demands and hectic pace of medicine, have I ignored the Almighty right before my eyes? Even more importantly, have I not seen God at work because I haven't been looking for him? Am I missing his presence, because (gulp), I don't expect him to be there?

I once heard Henry Blackaby say to a gathering of Christian doctors, "You will never see a patient that does not have God working somewhere in his or her life." Now anything that comes out of Henry Blackaby's mouth is bound to be profound, but that statement is a game changer. He added that, "maybe patients are coming to see you because God himself is drawing them." If these comments are true, then there is an enormous Gorilla loose in my office.

Spotting God at work requires two things. First, we need to develop the habit of looking for God in the lives of our patients. It will take practice to avoid just focusing on the physical and ignoring the spiritual. Second, we need to expect God to show up. Remember, inattentional blindness occurs in part when the object is unexpected. God may show up when and where and with the patients we would least expect him to. If we can "expect the unexpected" with God, we might just catch him in action more often.

Maybe this looks like pausing before going into an exam room and asking God to reveal what he is doing in the patient's life. Maybe it looks like questioning out loud with a patient whether all the trouble or heartache she is experiencing may be a sign that God is at work in her life. Maybe it looks like offering to pray for a patient before a surgery or during a difficult time. Whatever it takes, we need to train ourselves to look for him. There's no joy like sensing God's movement and being a part of the process as God draws someone to himself. Those moments provide huge surges of spiritual energy and give deep, transcendent meaning to the practice of medicine. And while sometimes God allows those opportunities to fall into our laps, often we need to be alert to spot them.

The biblical character Jacob, a forefather of the nation of Israel, suffered from inattentional blindness too. A specialist at deception and saving his own rear, Jacob often missed God working in his life. One of his most well-known quotes came from a moment of clarity in Genesis 28: "Surely the Lord is in this place, and I was not aware of it."

I can happily report I was one of the 50 percent who saw the gorilla the first time I watched the research video. But I know my success rate is a lot lower in spotting God at work as I practice medicine. May we all peel our eyes away from our own agendas and become more aware of the Gorilla moving through our days and in the lives of our patients.

Questions for reflection

1. Did you see the gorilla the first time you saw the Selective Attention Test video? How do you react to the possibility that this happens spiritually as well?

2. What are the most common reasons you miss seeing God during your day?

3. What habit can you develop to use each day to remind you of God's presence?

Nine

Unexpected

It would be easy to write pages full of reflections from my first missions trip, a medical mission to Nicaragua. I travelled in 2010 with a team from Global Health Outreach, the mission arm of the Christian Medical and Dental Association. I could easily share about the personal impact of working with fifty-three other Americans as we provided medical care to Nicaraguans living near the small fishing town of Masachapa. I could write about how God used us to treat 2,500 patients that week in the 98-degree Central American heat. Better yet, I could testify to the Spirit's power as over one hundred Nicaraguans indicated a spiritual decision that week, including the two men I lead to Christ in the dilapidated school classroom that was my temporary office. I could share how my heart grew as I met the poorest of the poor and realized the Living Water is at once both universal and relevant.

Instead, you have to hear about the plane ride home.

It was still dark as I said goodbye to my week-long roommate and headed to the airport in the capital city of Managua. My flight home was crazy early—6:00 a.m.—but I figured I could sleep on the plane before reuniting with my family later in the day.

The plane was as full going home as it was coming to Nicaragua, my row of three seats occupied. I had the window seat. Next to me was a young woman with a medium build and a pleasant smile, probably in her twenties. On the aisle was a woman with long dark hair who looked to be over thirty. Although I doubt they knew each other, these two women quickly struck up a conversation and chatted lively as we took off and ascended into the predawn Central American sky. I didn't catch the topic of their conversation, but the woman on the aisle seemed to be dominating whatever conversation they were having. Not having the energy at 6:00 a.m. to join the debate, I propped my knees up on the seat in front of me, inched my body down in the coach class seat, and prepared to doze off quickly after only a few hours of rest the night before.

I couldn't sleep. Not that the conversation between my row-mates was keeping me awake—the discussion ended after about twenty minutes, and the dark-haired woman on the aisle was already asleep. I didn't know at the time why my eyes wouldn't close. Giving up on sleep for the moment, I sat up and looked over at the younger woman next to me. She was browsing through some sort of pamphlet. As I continued to glance at her reading material, I realized she was viewing information about Jehovah's Witnesses. Maybe the lack of sleep lowered my inhibitions; maybe the week of sharing the gospel with the Nicaraguans emboldened me; or maybe the Holy Spirit cut through the fatigue and prompted me. Whatever the reason, I turned to the young woman next to me and asked, "What are you reading?"

You never know how someone is going to respond to an offer of conversation on a plane. Some people clearly don't want to be bugged. Usually the closed eyes and ear buds give that away. Fortunately, the young woman was receptive and, even better, spoke English. She flipped the pamphlet over a couple times and told me with a distinctive German accent that a friend had given her the pamphlet while she was in Nicaragua. Turns out she was a German college student working in Nicaragua on a project for her social work degree. Unfortunately, back pain was forcing her home, by way of Atlanta where we were headed, to receive medical attention.

Sensing her willingness to talk, I asked the German student what she thought about the pamphlet's message. With surprising candor, she admitted she didn't know what to think about the pamphlet, or about religion in general. Without hesitation, she shared about her upbringing and described herself as an agnostic without saying as much.

What followed was one of those moments where I can truly say God spoke through me. I shared my understanding of the beliefs of Jehovah's Witnesses, but then spoke of why I thought these beliefs fell short. With her continued attention as we traveled north over the Western Caribbean Sea, I laid out the gospel message for her, noting how truly unique it was among all other religions, and how the Good News of Jesus satisfies a heart's deepest longings like nothing else can.

It would be a great ending if I could say the German student immediately fell on her knees, and, with tears in her eyes, accepted Jesus as her Savior at that moment. But I can't, because she didn't. (Kneeling would have been hard in the economy class row anyway.) Instead, she took a deep breath, obviously processing all she had heard. I felt I had said enough and so gave her some mental space. She asked several follow up questions, which I answered. Her questions weren't deflective like so many are, such as, "If the Bible is true, then why is it filled with so many errors?" No, her queries revealed a heart-level wrestling with spiritual truths. There was no doubt in my mind God was after this young woman, and in the process, he had filled my heart to overflowing at the joy of sharing about him with her. Nevertheless, I didn't feel I should push the conversation further.

The woman seated on the aisle who had been the conversation dominator woke up just as our conversation ended. I don't think that was coincidental.

It wasn't long before the pilot came over the intercom announcing our descent into Atlanta. Time flies when it's divine. Before we stowed away our personal items, I felt God nudging me one more time. I asked the German student if she would like a Bible to read. She said she was interested. The only Bible I had with me was one I had received twenty years prior, ironically at a mission conference in Chicago. I hated to give it up, as it was a keepsake from my college days, but how could I not give away a copy of God's Word I had received from a conference about sharing God's Word?

I bookmarked the gospel of John and encouraged her to start there. She thanked me and tucked the Bible into her backpack. That would be the last time I would see the German student and my beloved Bible. But it's encouraging to think the beat-up paperback is now somewhere in Germany.

The experience in Nicaragua and on the flight home taught me many things. Mission trips, especially medical missions, are great. Global Health Outreach is an amazing organization doing God's work in the neediest of countries. Check them out online and sign up for a trip. You can go even as a medical student or resident.

Yet God chose to use me most, not on what I thought was the "mission field" in Nicaragua, but when and where I least expected it. And he chose a time when I was least prepared. Why? To show me that sharing my faith is not about, "wise and persuasive words, but with a demonstration of the Spirit's power, so that your faith might not rest on human wisdom, but on God's power" (1 Corinthians 2:4-5). He picked a time when I am not normally coherent so

I wouldn't depend on my own strength, but on his. Left to myself, I would have fallen asleep and totally missed this divine appointment. It was God who put the German student in the seat next to me, God who kept me awake, God who kept the aisle-seated woman asleep during the entire conversation, God who spoke to the student through me, and it continues to be God who, I'm convinced, is still working in her heart today. All I did was show up for the flight.

Asking questions is a great way to begin a conversation about anything, let alone spiritual truths. It was one of Jesus' favorite tools when he was here. People love to talk about themselves, and questions can start off a conversation in a less-threatening way. Since that airplane conversation, I have learned to lead off with questions if I want to start spiritual conversations with patients.

I also was reminded on the flight that sharing my faith is not about seeing results. It is about being obedient to God. I don't know if the German student ever accepted Christ. I still pray to this day she does. But on that flight, I was called to simply share the Good News. That's it. Seeds were planted at thirty thousand feet that morning. It's God's job to grow that seed into faith.

The Apostle Peter wrote, "Always be prepared to give an answer to everyone who asks you to give the reason for the hope that you have" (1 Peter 3:15). God might just nudge you when you least expect it. Are you ready?

Questions for reflection

1. Have you had a chance to share your faith? What was it like? How did you feel God's nudging? What fears surfaced along the way?

2. Do you feel you are prepared to give an answer to everyone who asks you to give the reason for the hope that you have? While God will certainly speak through you, Peter encourages us to be prepared. A helpful practice is to write out your testimony of how God saved you and the difference he has made in your life since then. Consider writing it down on your next day off. If you have already done so, maybe it's time to pull out the testimony to refresh your memory of God's faithfulness.

3. When could you take a medical missions trip? What might God teach you through an experience like that?

Ten

A headful

I could have stayed a student forever. Okay, maybe not a medical student, with the volume of information flooding the brain during those years, but perhaps a college student. I could hang out on campus full time, taking courses that would interest me now like Revolutionary War History or Film Production, or even off-the-wall courses like UFOs in American Society offered at Temple or The Physics of Superheroes at the University of Minnesota. What fun it would be to quit my job and sit back and just soak in all that information all day—until my wife calls to tell me the electric has been shut off at home.

I enjoy learning. Discovering new information fascinates me. And if you are in the medical field, I suspect you feel the same. The training for our profession is too arduous and the learning too lifelong to tolerate if you are not a student at heart. The acquisition of medical knowledge may be one factor that drew many of us to the field. And so, it would follow that we derive a certain satisfaction from the accumulation of that knowledge. It sounds nerdy, I know, but isn't it true? Who hasn't felt more confident after acing a renal physiology exam or surged with pride after impressing an attending with a medical fact you happened to read the night before?

Gathering knowledge can be satisfying and stimulating, but it comes with an inherent flaw. I remember my Residency Director's excitement when our program matched with a student from an Ivy

League medical school for the first time. He almost burst with anticipation to watch her put that top-notch education into practice at his residency. Indeed, the Ivy Leaguer did arrive with a great fund of knowledge. No doubt her education had been fantastic. But from the start she struggled mightily to apply that headful of information to real-world medicine. For some reason, she couldn't translate her knowledge into managing patients. Differential diagnoses paralyzed her. She saw too many zebras and didn't know how to find the horses. Despite intensive support from faculty and fellow residents, she never grasped the art of primary care and left the residency.

Accumulating spiritual knowledge can have the same result. It's tempting to read God's Word simply to gather information about our faith. We can open our minds to the truths of God, but often those insights never leave our skull. Despite a headful of spiritual knowledge, we can struggle like the Ivy Leaguer to apply it to real-world living.

Here's a recent example from my life. One morning for my devotions I turn to Isaiah 40. I read:

28 Do you not know?

Have you not heard?

The LORD is the everlasting God,

the Creator of the ends of the earth.

He will not grow tired or weary,

and his understanding no one can fathom.

29 He gives strength to the weary

and increases the power of the weak.

30 Even youths grow tired and weary,

and young men stumble and fall;

31 but those who hope in the LORD

will renew their strength.

They will soar on wings like eagles;

they will run and not grow weary,

they will walk and not be faint.

The passage is familiar; I even know a song with the words. But I determine to see it afresh today. As I study and meditate on the passage, my eyes glance down to the NIV study notes at the bottom of the page. I notice a comment about the word "renew" from verse 31. The study notes state this word literally means "exchange." This is new information to me, and my pulse quickens with the insight. It's easy as Christians to say we are trusting in God for strength, but how often do we end up still trying to accomplish it all by ourselves? I conclude that it's not about pulling ourselves up by our spiritual boot straps, but loosening our grip on and emptying ourselves of our inadequate strength so God can exchange it for his. Pleased with the new information I have learned, I utter a barely audible *huh!* Somewhere in the back of my mind I tell myself to remember this insight, as it may come in handy at small group or Sunday school. I close my Bible, say a quick prayer for my day, and I'm off to work.

A few days later, I wonder in frustration why I don't have the strength to pull myself out of a burned-out, short-fused, compassion-less funk.

Paul gives a great word picture in 1 Corinthians that speaks to the issue of knowledge accumulation:

> We know that we all possess knowledge. Knowledge puffs up, but love builds up. The man who thinks he knows something does not yet know as he ought to know. But the man who loves God is known by God.
>
> 1 Corinthians: 8:1-3.

Information is great. The satisfaction I feel from learning new things is God-given. But my life will be as substantial as a balloon if I pursue spiritual knowledge as an end in itself. If not applied in my life through loving God and loving others, information gained from scripture like the passage in Isaiah is useless. Thus, the step I thought I took toward Christlikeness that morning was actually a step backwards toward shallowness and pride.

Author A.W. Tozer extends this thought even further. He would argue that I had never gained any insight from the Isaiah passage in the first place. Tozer wrote, "Truth, to be understood, must be lived." It's in the application of God's Word through acts of love that I truly gain knowledge and grow to be a built-up, substantial Christian. Along the way I don't just fill mental filing cabinets with spiritual insights—I grow in my relationship with God.

Let's go even one step further. The Bible, God's Word, is a *Living* Word that searches us. Hebrews 4:12 says it best: "For the word of God is alive and active. Sharper than any double-edged sword, it penetrates even to dividing soul and spirit, joints and marrow; it judges the thoughts and attitudes of the heart." Author Tim Keller says the Bible is the way that, through the Spirit, God is active in our lives. This is what separates the Bible from every other book written. I've heard it said that we don't just read the Bible, it reads us. Through his Spirit, God animates the inked pages of a book written thousands of years ago and uses them to accomplish his purposes in our lives.

It would be wise for those of us in medicine to recognize the propensity for treating God's Word like an issue of JAMA. So how do I know if I am properly applying God's Word? How do I know if I have allowed the Living Word to penetrate my soul and spirit? It's a simple query that can be answered by asking myself some equally simple but sobering questions:

Am I more patient after studying about patience in scripture?
Does my heart ache more for the poor after reading Isaiah 58?
Do I complain less after reading about the Crucifixion?
Am I treating that difficult co-worker differently after reading the Sermon on the Mount?

In the end, I will probably not be remembered as a doctor for my medical knowledge. I will be remembered by patients and coworkers for the level of *care* in my medical care. Likewise, when I stand before God on Judgement Day, my life will be evaluated not on the amount of spiritual information I have packed into my brain, but on the amount of love that has flowed out of my heart.

Questions for reflection

1. What college courses would you take if you could go back?

2. How have you seen the tendency for knowledge to puff you up?

3. What would it look like to let scripture search your heart?

4. What could you read in the Bible this week that you could then attempt to live out?

Eleven

The monk and the four-eyed fish: a half-fable

Once long ago there was a monk who lived at a monastery in France. His name was Nicholas but for some reason the other monks called him Larry. Now Larry had entered the monastery when he was twenty-six years old, after having lived an unexceptional life to that point: born into a poor family, Larry only completed elementary school, later joined the army but was injured in war, and afterward failed in the world of finance after breaking too many of his boss' personal possessions. But along the way this clumsy, uneducated oaf found God and decided that sacrificing his life to him as a monk might pay for his faults and failures.

Upon joining the monastery, Larry was assigned kitchen duty. Really, what else was there for a newbie monk who didn't know Latin? The kitchen was a busy place, often full of hustle and bustle, which is a testament not only to the number of monks Larry lived with but also their ability to eat. Larry greatly disliked kitchen work, and in the early years of monastic life he struggled—with doubt, guilt, and even with the assurance of his salvation.

One particularly bad day in those early years, Larry did what most monks do when they are frustrated: he went fishing. Gathering up his pole and bait, Larry lumbered a mile or two down the well-traveled road near the monastery, turning onto a narrow path that led to a secluded river he had frequented before. The day was especially bright, and a crisp freshness hung in the spring air as Larry settled upon a new section in a bend of the river to fish.

After fumbling to set the hook, he tossed the line to the middle of the river, the bait settling on the water's surface. As he sat, Larry's mind flowed with questions. How had his life turned out this way? Why would God place him in a kitchen of all places? How could God possibly use him while peeling potatoes for the evening stew? But then again what did he have to offer God? Why would God want to use him? Only the murmuring of the river water as it passed over well-worn rocks provided any response.

Just then the fishing line tightened, almost jerking the rod out of Larry's hands. His whirling thoughts suddenly ceased as he gripped the arching pole and began wrestling the line. The fish was putting up a marvelous fight; twice Larry almost lost the pole before he finally won the battle and hoisted the catch out of the water.

Immediately Larry knew something was different about the fish he had caught. Never before had he seen such a strange creature. The body was fish-like, slender and adorned with the usual fins. But the eyes—it was the fish's eyes that caught his attention. It looked to Larry that each of the fish's eyes were actually two, with an eye stacked on top of another, like two soap bubbles joined together. Larry would have thought the fish looked like something out of a failed genetic experiment, but fellow monk Gregor Mendel and his peas wouldn't arrive on the scene for another two hundred years.

"You're a feisty one, if not a bit peculiar looking," Larry muttered out loud, carefully removing the hook from the fish's mouth.

At once the four-eyed fish turned its head, looked straight at the monk, and replied, "Shall I take that as a compliment?"

Larry stumbled back upon hearing this voice, let alone coming from a fish, almost dropping the scaled wonder. A talking fish? Had he inhaled too much smoke in the kitchen? Was a head injury from the war just now showing up? Larry waited a moment to see if he would wake up from this odd dream. He did not. He concluded the moment must be real indeed and he continued to stare speechless at the miraculous fish staring back at him.

After several moments, Larry suddenly remembered his monk-ish manners and realized it was rude of him not to respond to the fish's inquiry.

"Why, y-y-yes . . . my apologies . . . you can talk!?!? And your eyes, they are just . . . so unique! I have never seen anything quite like them before!"

"Well, they are not there by accident," replied the fish, "and while I admit their appearance is unusual, they are perfectly suited to the way I was created to live. You see, kind sir, I spend most of my days at the surface of the water. My lower eyes keep watch for predators in the waters below who would do me harm, while my upper eyes look for tasty morsels skimming across the water surface. I much prefer those creatures you call insects to what I can find below. Besides, the air-breathing creatures are much lower in cholesterol."

"So you peer above and below the surface of the water at the same time?" questioned the monk, now intensely curious about this four-eyed fish.

"Yes indeed," stated the fish proudly, "I see both worlds in one moment. In fact, the two are one reality to me. I live in both simultaneously."

Suddenly Larry realized this fish was sent by God to answer the questions that plagued him for so long. *Two worlds, one reality.* Maybe that was the secret he had been looking for. In essence, his personal struggles centered on trying to integrate the secular, commonplace side of life with the spiritual. The kitchen and the chapel may be just down the hall from each other at the monastery, but his activities in them seemed worlds apart. Would it be possible for him to join these two worlds together in one reality? Could he live perpetually in the spiritual, enjoying the presence of God even while he was busy with his kitchen duties? Could his secular and spiritual activities be joined into singular acts of love before God? He was determined to find out.

As is true of most fables, this short story has an animal as a central character and a moral to convey. But I labelled this a *half-fable* because, while no fish can obviously speak French, the monk and the four-eyed fish nevertheless are real. And we have much to learn from them.

Found in the freshwater rivers of Central and South America, the four-eyed fish deserves the "Hey, look at four eyes!" taunts from other fish. Two eyes adorn each side of its head, stacked vertically like the headlights on a '67 Pontiac GTO. The appearance is both bizarre and strangely fascinating. (If you want to get technical, the fish only has two eyes. Each eye has two pupils, giving the appearance of two eyes set vertically, but the eyes share a common lens, retina, and optic nerve.) Regardless of the anatomy, let's just say this fish does not need a Halloween costume.

The four-eyed fish is not a two-eyed fish that just rapidly switches its attention from the world above the water to the world below, back and forth. No, the fish collects information from both worlds simultaneously and its little fish brain integrates the information together. The little fish has two worlds, but one reality.

This otherwise obscure aquatic creature provides a great image of how Christians are to "see" their world. With the empowerment of the Holy Spirit, we have the ability to view the spiritual and physical realms simultaneously. As I go about my day perceiving the physical world with my five senses, below the surface of my soul operates another set of "eyes," spiritual ones that give me the potential to sense God's movement and promptings. Two worlds, but one reality.

But how do we do this? Like the fish, we are not meant to be two-eyed Christians that quickly switch our attention between the sacred and secular. We are to live four-eyed. But how?

This was the question our other story character, a real seventeenth century French monk named Brother Lawrence, struggled with for forty years. He wrestled with integrating his spiritual and physical worlds, the sacred and secular, into one. His first decade of monastic life was rough—he frequently stumbled over the depths of his sin and feelings of unworthiness before God. Yet Brother Lawrence assiduously clung to a practice that would revolutionize his life and ultimately the lives of many who followed his example in centuries to come.

And though he would have likely never seen one, Brother Lawrence sought to practice what the four-eyed fish lives naturally: to make one reality out of two worlds. In his search, he came upon a simple formula. Brother Lawrence simply thought of God often. Before he began his day, Brother Lawrence prayed that God would grant him grace to remain in his presence all day. He then proceeded throughout the day to continue in conversation with God, asking for his grace, and offering him all his actions. With a little remembrance of God here, one brief act of inward worship there, Brother Lawrence peppered his day with God. He strove to do nothing and think nothing that would displease his Heavenly Father. Diligently he drove away everything from his mind that was capable of interrupting his thoughts of God. When his mind wandered, out of necessity from his work or involuntarily, he would simply bring his thoughts back to God, sensing God's loving tug on his heart to return his focus on him.

The result? After years of this practice, Brother Lawrence reached a point where he was able to write:

> For me, work time is no different than prayer time.
> Even in the noise and clatter of the kitchen, with different people calling for different things all at once, I still know God's presence with just as much real peace as if I were on my knees at communion.

This simple monk arrived at a place where it was difficult for him *not* to think of God all the time. God's presence flowed in his life continuously, naturally, effortlessly. Rather than distracting him from his work in the kitchen, Brother Lawrence believed God's presence aided him in his duties. And he discovered that the habits he developed led to a trifecta of rewards: "an unclouded vision, an illumined love, a joy uninterrupted."

After his death, Brother Lawrence's letters and writings were assembled into a book by a friend. *The Practice of the Presence of God* would become one of the most important Christian books ever written.

I know I'm biased, but it seems to me that the field of medicine makes this two worlds-one reality stuff harder than in most professions. Whether in training or out in practice, the days are so hectic, the information so voluminous, and the responsibilities so weighty that it's easy to forget about God. It's easy to live with God is relegated to a small section of my week, comprised of Sunday mornings (before one o'clock during football season) and the occasional ten-minute morning devotion. Too often the bulk of my week is, to be honest, God-less.

Can you relate to what one first-year medical student wrote?

> I often feel I have so little space in my mind and so little
> strength to offer. Is it a valid thought to think that God
> understands where I'm at, he doesn't expect me to have
> more to offer him right now?

Somehow, practicing the presence of God needs to not be the intellectual property of a dead monk from centuries ago or the rare spiritual giant among us, but for all, even during medical school or while doing Q2 call. But how? Achieving what Brother Lawrence did seems so daunting, so overwhelming, that we might give up before we try. Brother Lawrence would tell us we are making it too hard. He would tell us how he searched books and received advice from spiritual mentors about living in God's presence but none of it was as helpful as when he committed to simply thinking a thought about God. And then doing it again. And again. And again.

Sure, Brother Lawrence struggled his first decade in the monastery and described his early practice of God's presence as "no small pain," but he would tell us any struggling he experienced was his own doing. God wasn't the one who was distant, or whose mind

61

wandered, or whose doubt entangled. It was only after he got over himself that Brother Lawrence was able to recognize and enjoy the presence of the One who was there all along.

———————————————

All fables have a moral, and this one is no exception. It's best summed up by the author A.W. Tozer, a contemporary and admirer of Brother Lawrence. Tozer wrote, "Let us believe that God is in all our simple deeds and learn to find him there."

The process of finding God in those simple deeds starts with thinking a thought about God. And it ultimately can lead to a life lived as naturally as a four-eyed fish or as powerfully as a simple French monk.

Questions for reflection

1. How do you relate to the quote from the first-year medical student above?

2. It took Brother Lawrence years to develop the habits and disciplines that led him so deeply and constantly into God's presence. What can you do this week to start on that path?

Twelve

The good lawyer:
An adaptation of Luke 10

A certain man set out on a journey down the road of his life. Along the way, he fell into the hands of robbers—Divorce, Unemployment, and Depression. They stripped him of his identity, beat him and went away, leaving his spirit half-dead.

A family physician happened to be going down the same road, and came upon the man. When he saw him, the physician realized he was thirty minutes behind schedule, so he gave him a prescription for some lingering cold symptoms and passed by on the other side.

So too, a specialist, when he came upon the man, reminded himself of the narrow scope of his training. He ordered a panel of expensive blood work and passed by on the other side.

But a malpractice lawyer came to where the man was; when he saw him, he took pity on him. He went to the man, and realizing the true nature of his injuries, treated his wounds, pouring on empathy and compassion. Then he arranged further care for the man and followed up on his recovery.

Which of these three do you think was a healer to the man who fell into the hands of robbers?

The one who had mercy on him.

Go and do likewise.

Questions for reflection

1. What do the actions of the family physician and the specialist in the parable reveal about their hearts?

2. What prevents you from realizing the true nature of your patient's "injuries"?

3. Proverbs 20:5 says, "The purposes of a person's heart are deep waters, but one who has insight draws them out." What steps could you take this week to step into the deep waters of your patients' lives and draw them out?

Thirteen

You had me at hello

Someone's face lights up when they see you walk into a room.

Teams are being chosen and the captains are fighting over you.

A cross-country friend remembers to call on your birthday.

A classmate texts, checking on your recovery from an illness.

Feels good, doesn't it? We like being noticed and celebrated. We love to be loved. We appreciate being appreciated. It's human nature.

So here's a question: How do patients feel when they step out of the exam room after their visit with you? Do they feel valued? Do they feel heard? Do they feel cared for? Or do they feel judged? Rushed? Ignored? I know it may seem we're about to launch into a hokey customer service lecture. But remember the times when someone made that extra effort for you and how it felt. Contrast those experiences with the times you were treated like a number and the taste left in your mouth.

Recently I visited a local eye doctor for a check-up. From the robotic, no-eye-contact greeting of the receptionist to the hurried handshake goodbye from the doctor, I felt rushed and anonymous (and they knew I was a physician!). Despite receiving solid ophthalmologic care from a competent professional utilizing the latest technology, I left unsatisfied. The result? I have been recommending other eye doctors to my patients.

Twenty-five patient visits a day . . . five days a week . . . fifty weeks a year . . . for thirty years adds up to nearly two hundred thousand patient encounters in a primary care career. The numbers may not be far off in a specialty or surgical field. Such a constant stream of people will erode your relational edge. Think about the patients you saw this past week, whether in a residency clinic, the ED or ICU. Did you take time for introductions, seeking to learn something about the fellow human in front of you? Did you notice the new hairstyle she sported or the weight loss he finally achieved? Did you investigate the patient's hidden agenda? Were you looking at the computer screen more than the patient? Did you seize the little opportunities to offer an empathic statement or comforting hand on the shoulder? Too often during office hours my mind is one patient ahead or my thoughts in a jumbled rush as I walk into an exam room, and the visit is lukewarm, distracted, even mechanical. I fool myself if I think patients don't care. They do.

A specialist I shadowed during residency was the poster child for pitiful patient interaction. He would burst into an exam room without knocking—startling most patients—and launch into a discussion even before he sat down. Introductions? No time. Small talk? What's that? The patients' reactions were predictable: if they didn't suffer cardiac arrest from his explosive entrance, they struggled to put aside their agenda and jump onto his train of thought as it raced past. Throughout the visit, the specialist's eyes were glued to the patient's chart as if he were reading a Grisham novel. The exam was brief and sudden. Then without warning, he would rise and bolt out of the exam room, leaving the patient and me staring at each other in disbelief at what had just occurred. After several similar episodes, I learned to tell patients in a hushed voice, "I think your visit is finished."

Out in the real world, you will be scored and paid based on patient satisfaction, so this stuff is relevant. But for Christians, we're talking about something much bigger than just good customer service. My attitude, my words, my tone, my concern—they're all a reflection of something deeper going on inside me. If there is one point to draw out of Jesus' Sermon on the Mount (and there are many), it's that the outer self reveals the inner self, the state of the heart. Throughout scripture, God makes it clear that outward actions are important, though not just as an end to themselves, but as a peek behind the curtain at the heart motives hidden backstage.

In light of this, what should be our heart attitude toward the infirm under our care? What should fuel our compassion each day? What is our responsibility to the countless people we meet? Is there a good rule of thumb we can rely on to guide our hearts?

Treating every patient as if he is your rich uncle from whom you stand to inherit millions may be a good motivator, but won't pay off your student loans.

Honoring each patient because some have "entertained angels" without knowing it may get you a little further—until you grow tired of not spotting any halos.

But the simple principle of *treating patients as you would want to be treated* will sustain you for the long haul. And it's, well, golden.

Jesus hit a homerun when he boiled down our responsibility to our fellow man in this aureate command. The genius in the Golden Rule is that it's at once both stunningly succinct and yet inexhaustibly comprehensive. There are no qualifiers to consider, no multipliers to confuse, no expressions to simplify. How I want to be treated should equal how I treat others. It's that simple.

But maybe it's not. Because I expect so much from others with how they treat me, I set the bar unobtainably high for my behavior toward others. There are no minimal requirements I can complete to satisfy the demands of the Golden Rule because my need for love, respect, appreciation, patience, grace, forgiveness, understanding, and kindness from others is an unquenchable fire. I'll never get away with treating others poorly because I would never tolerate that behavior toward myself.

But let's face it. Gandhi or Desmond Tutu or even Shrek could have uttered the Golden Rule and it would have been just as significant. Yet the fact it came from Jesus, who came from heaven and sacrificed his life to show his love for us, adds another dimension to our responsibility toward others. Now, because of the cross, not only should I do to others as I would have done to me, I should do to others *because of what God has done for me.* Jesus' life and sacrifice supercharge the Golden Rule, upgrading it from brilliant ethical code to life-surrendering thankfulness.

Despite the craziness that is the practice of medicine, it's wise to stop periodically and take your pulse—your relational pulse. How well are your treating others? How gracious is your bedside manner? Are you applying the same compassion and attention toward your patients you would expect if it was you in that hospital bed? Do your words and actions reflect your gratitude for Jesus' sacrifice for you? It all matters to God, even the simplest of conversations and smallest of acts, and so it should matter to us. Why? Because of what our words and actions reveal about our hearts.

Questions for reflection

1. Have you had a recent experience being a patient? How you were treated? How did it feel? What did you learn from being on the other side?

2. Jesus said, "whoever has been forgiven little loves little" (Luke 7:47). What does your attitude toward your medical school class-mates or toward patients reveal about your understanding of God's forgiveness in your life?

3. Who can you show supercharged-Golden-Rule love to this week?

Fourteen

Can you hear me now?

Twenty-seven miles southeast of Lancaster, Pennsylvania, near the Delaware state line, my favorite radio station is dying. Static infests the songs on WJTL as I weave and climb then plunge on Route 896 toward the college town of Newark. Eventually, there's nothing recognizable in the moth-eaten music and I must hunt a new station. Farms and small towns blanket the landscape along this road, so the radio scanner offers only a handful of options as it circles. I'll listen to the strongest signal, even though it's playing Toby Keith, because I know it won't be long before this station will succumb like my favorite.

I'm too cheap to buy satellite radio, but it sure sounds tempting—digital space rays beaming seamless radio coverage coast to coast. The power of satellite radio is in the height of the transmitter. Twenty-two thousand miles above the equator, floating hunks of aluminum shower E minor chords and drum beats into a god-like omnipresence. Anywhere there's a clear shot to the sky, the signal is constant, immediate, and pervasive.

Not so with standard radio. The height of the transmitter is its weakness. Try a meager 2,723 feet for the world's tallest radio tower (and it's not in the U.S.). Add a couple hills and a few dozen miles, and you'll be listening to Toby Keith too.

My car radio and I are wired alike. We both process messages received from the outside world, resulting in some sort of action.

The electronic brick tucked in my car dashboard decodes electro-magnetic waves to fill the car with voice and music. Every day messages stream toward me from many sources—media, popular culture, a parent or coworker, the next-door neighbor—which are picked up by the internal receiver located somewhere between my ears. These messages trickle their way down into my wiring where they are decoded and processed. Some may be immediately deleted, especially if I am not paying attention, but more often than not, most messages carry enough power to alter my course to the subtlest degree. Opinions may be formed, or ideas generated. Priorities may be shifted, or beliefs influenced. Those external messages shape who I am.

But these aren't satellite messages. Endure a little hardship, grow a few years older, climb several peaks or endure a few valleys, and you'll hear static in those signals. Eventually the messages fade—once so clear and robust, once holding such weight and veracity in your life. You'll soon realize the transmitters you've been relying on to guide you are earth-bound and makeshift. And so your hunt will begin again. Before you know it, you'll discover much of your life has been spent bouncing from one message to another, endlessly searching, scanning for another to fill the air.

God's Word is the satellite signal for our souls. Its power is in the height of the Source. The Holy and Transcendent Creator showers a message with enough spiritual wattage to reach the furthest heart. The signal is constant, immediate, and pervasive. No difficult circumstance, no length of time, no shift in cultural ideology, not even the furthest moral distance can diminish the message. In fact, the signal is often the strongest in the darkest and most remote places a heart must travel. Maybe that's because all other messages have faded out by then.

It's good practice to regularly evaluate your signal sources. Running a quick set of diagnostics will do: What are the priorities in your life? What do you fear? In what do you find your identity? How do you spend your free time? How much of your day is spent in self-preservation? The answers to these seemingly unrelated queries will indicate the source of the signals you receive.

In this world of a million messages vying for our attention, where can we find a reliable source to lock our presets to?

Look higher.

Questions for reflection

1. Ask yourself the reflective questions above. (Answer them honestly, not with what you think are the correct "Christian" answers). What do your answers reveal about God's place in your life?

2. How many of your answers are based on the eternal, satellite-signal promises found in God's Word? Why aren't the others?

3. Pick one of those questions to reflect on this week. What would it take to change the answer?

Fifteen

Temple dwelling

On October 6, 2013, the NBC's *Today* show lost one of its most enduring members. It wasn't an anchor or a member of the broadcast team, not even someone on the payroll. Linny Boyette stood in the crowd outside the Rockefeller Center show almost daily—for nearly twenty years. Enduring an hour-long commute from the Bronx, Linny rarely missed a weekday broadcast until his death in 2013. He was considered the *Today* show's ultimate fan. His sister thought he was mental.

In the 1970s and '80s, Rollen Stewart frequented sporting events across the country, famous for his rainbow-colored Afro wig and cardboard sign advertising John 3:16. Through the years he was spotted at NFL, MLB and NBA games, the Indianapolis 500, and even the Olympics. For an unrelated reason, he's been in prison since 1992.

It's not a stretch to say the type of behavior exhibited by these two men, although dedicated, could be construed as a bit wacky. So when I read about an obscure New Testament character acting similarly, forgive me for thinking she's missing a few marbles.

Ever the detail-oriented physician, the gospel writer Luke introduces us to Anna the Prophetess in Luke 2 like he's reading her medical chart: "Eighty-four-year-old woman, the daughter of Phanuel, of the tribe of Asher. Widowed after six years of marriage, never remarried." Nothing noteworthy so far. But then Luke reports a stunning fact about this woman. He writes, "She never left the temple but worshiped night and day, fasting and praying." Now this wasn't just a three-day women's retreat or a week-long revival meeting. Luke gives us a few numbers and lets us do the math: Anna may have remained at the temple for over sixty years. Some scholars think Anna lived at the temple. Whether she commuted there each morning or hit the snooze button not far from the Holy of Holies, you've gotta admit six decades of temple dwelling goes beyond dedication and is even more fanatical than Linny or Rollen.

And yet before we write off Anna's actions as kooky and extreme, notice the last scene of her brief biblical story: the day she meets the child Jesus and his parents in the temple during his dedication.

> Coming up to them at that very moment, [Anna] gave
> thanks to God and spoke about the child to all who
> were looking forward to the redemption of Jerusalem.
>
> Luke 2:38

For all her insane dedication, there's no getting around the fact that Anna was one of only a few people on the face of the earth at that moment who recognized Jesus' significance. Biblical experts and Teachers of the Law probably walked right past Jesus in the temple courts that day, failing to notice the promised Messiah sleeping in Mary's arms. How did this obscure widow spot him? Spending sixty years in the presence of God has its benefits. With that amount of God-exposure, Anna could easily recognize him when he came through the door. Anna would have been constantly awaiting and looking for Jesus, and she finally found him that day.

We can argue that it was easy for Anna to worship God full-time—she didn't do anything else all day. And yet I was struck by the thought that Anna's story is in the Bible not for page filler, but for good reason. Certainly her testimony about Jesus gives credence to his deity. But is it possible that Luke also included Anna's story as an example for us to follow? Could it be that we are called to live like Anna and never leave the temple too? But how? Do we need to quit medicine and become monks and nuns? (I did hear about a monastery in New Hampshire advertising on Facebook.)

Like so many other principles in scripture, God is not looking primarily for a change in our external activity, but rather a transformation of our hearts. But yet again the protests arise quickly in our minds: how is it possible for us, as overworked medical professionals, to figuratively never leave the temple, to worship God night and day like Anna? Our mental energy and focus is finite—so how do we find the capacity to do this? The challenge is to somehow foster an inner atmosphere of joyful worship before our creator while we go about our daily lives. We must create within ourselves a quiet place where prayers and thoughts are being lifted to God, even while we are studying for an exam, working on an H&P, closing an abdominal surgical site, or reading an x-ray. How is this possible?

Put God at the center. Sinclair Ferguson wrote, "Where God is at the center of things, worship inevitably follows." When God is on the throne of my heart, he becomes my reference point. I see others as created in his image and deeply loved by him. I realize my circumstances as the unfolding of his perfect will. I view the human body as wondrously designed by an expert craftsman. I marvel at creation as a beautiful and orderly testimony to his presence. My heart cannot help but worship the One who is through all and in all. There is only one throne in my heart. I will worship whomever or whatever occupies the seat.

Reflect often on God. Where does your mind run to when you have a spare moment? Train it to think about God. Let him fill your thoughts. When you get a chance, look back at Psalm 63, near the front of this book. Don't you get the impression that David was almost obsessed with God? He's up, "through the watches of the night," not unlike a med student cramming for an exam or a resident writing a midnight admission note. The difference is, David was up thinking about God. It's not a stretch to say the Lord was always on his mind, despite being chased by Saul or attending to his duties as king. In fact, I suspect it was the times David wasn't thinking much about God that he got into trouble, like with his female neighbor Bathsheba (detailed in 2 Samuel 11). A.W. Tozer once suggested a great practice: lift up a thousand thought-prayers to the Lord every day as you go about the job of living.

Do everything for his glory. Paul wrote in 1 Corinthians that even our eating and drinking, the most common acts we perform as humans, should be done to the glory of God. The inspiration, motivation, and goal of all we do should be not to advance ourselves but to make much of God. Worship will flow naturally out of a heart that is dedicated to seeing him magnified.

By putting God on the throne of our lives, by reflecting often on him, and by doing everything for his glory, we can become temple dwellers like Anna. The result? We will recognize when God walks through the front door.

Questions for reflection

1. Think about someone you know who is fanatical about
something (it could be yourself). Maybe it's an obsession about a
sports team, or a hobby, or social media. Describe the obsession.
What fuels it? What behaviors characterize it? What benefits does
it have? What does it cost?

2. If you're honest, who or what sits on the throne of your heart
right now? What steps do you need to take this week to dethrone it
and place God there?

3. What would it take for you to lift up a thousand thought-
prayers to God each day?

Sixteen

The least of these

Family Healthers. It's what we called the patients of our family medicine residency clinic when I was in training. The patients were poor. They were on welfare. They were ethnicities we were not. Hearing the phrase *Family Healther* would immediately stir in any resident's mind the image of an underachieving, histrionic, pregnant teenager who drags her child to the ER at 3:00 a.m. for a diaper rash and yet shows up an hour late for her clinic visit demanding to be seen.

I am convinced that, had Jesus come to my town instead of Israel two thousand years ago, the Family Healthers would be the people he would have sought out. The fatherless. The homeless. The HIV positive. The modern-day lepers and "sinners" of Jesus' day. They were the *least of these* he referred to during his ministry, detailed in Matthew 25.

Using a stinging allegory to make his point, Jesus identified the lowest of the low in society—the hungry, the thirsty, the strangers, the unclothed, the sick, the imprisoned—and then linked himself directly to them. "Whatever you did for one of the least of these brothers and sisters of mine, you did for me" (Matthew 25:40).

Had Jesus been in my residency class, he wouldn't have just fulfilled the minimal requirements with these patients. He would have loved them, lived with them, ate with them, laughed with them, shared his life with them, given his life for them. It's who he came for and who he was drawn to.

It's nice to think Jesus would have befriended me had he come to town. After all, I am a physician. Wouldn't I, as a medical professional, have been a valuable asset as one of his disciples? We would have made a great team working side by side tending to the sick. I wouldn't have scratched my head when he told a parable. I wouldn't have doubted if he called me out of the boat—I've water skied before! I wouldn't have betrayed him. I wouldn't have run away when he was arrested. Right?

The reality is that I am more like the rich young ruler of Mark 10, who came to Jesus looking for back-slapping affirmation of his obedience but left with a butt-kicking conviction of loving his wealth too much. Jesus would have easily seen through my status to reveal my self-promoting motives and sent me packing as well. Then he would have returned to caring for the Family Healthers.

Why them? Because they are the folk described in his mission statement:

> The Spirit of the Lord is on me,
>
> because he has anointed me
>
> to proclaim good news to the poor.
>
> He has sent me to proclaim freedom for the prisoners
>
> and recovery of sight for the blind,
>
> to set the oppressed free,
>
> to proclaim the year of the Lord's favor.

> Luke 4:14-21

Unless I am missing something, nowhere does that passage mention him coming for the proud and self-sufficient.

Who are the Family Healthers at your hospital or clinic? Seek them out, just as Jesus did in his time. As David Loxtercamp stated so well in JAMA: "Doctors rise to their best by serving the least of their patients—the least insured, the least curable, the least attractive, responsible, or grateful. The least like us."

Why is this true? Because we look like our Savior when we do.

Questions for reflection

1. Jesus saw the care of the poor and oppressed, the hungry and thirsty, not as extra credit, but as proof of a life surrendered to God. What does your level of care and compassion for these people reveal about your spiritual maturity?

2. Who are the *least of these* in your practice or hospital? What is your impression of them from recent interactions? How can you see them as God does? What could you do this week to seek them out?

3. Pray that God would give you a greater heart and compassion for those least like you.

Seventeen

Hopkins and me

During the lunch break of a pediatrics conference at Johns Hopkins, I sense a need to restore blood flow to my legs before a long afternoon session. Finding an exit, I step outside. Although I squint on a cloudless day anticipating sunlight will overload my eyes, none hits my face. The buildings on this street are tight and tall, almost bending over to form a canopy, hindering the sun. For most of the break I wander around in the shadows of this hallowed medical university, trying to look like I belong. The stately Billings Administration building, with its dome five stories high, sits like an ancient red-brick cathedral in the campus center. A ten-foot Jesus stands inside the building's lofty rotunda. Several other elderly structures have their names chiseled into the stone, high above the entrances. The spelling is peculiar, betraying the age of these Monuments of Medicine. It's as if the intention of these lofty inscriptions is to cause those who dare come near to gaze at the grandeur of the whole building, finishing in an almost worshipful pose, before the name is finally revealed. It is to awe as much as to inform.

The effect worked. Having listened to distinguished Hopkins faculty all morning and now engulfed by these stone and brick Forefathers, I sense an emotion within I have not felt since the first few days of internship: intimidation. I am a young family physician fresh out of residency. I work in a private practice in a nondescript Pennsylvania suburb. This is Johns Hopkins! Why am I caring for patients? I should just post Google directions to Baltimore on my office door. I stand paralyzed on the sidewalk, lost in obsessive thought, my confidence hemorrhaging like an arterial bleed. In an intellectual panic, I quickly recite a few medical facts to recover my confidence (really, I did). But this exercise backfires when I realize the facts I recall were from the morning lectures I just heard. I'm hopeless.

Then I remember a recent patient visit. A man scheduled with me to have his ear wax flushed. He told me the week before he had made a pilgrimage to Johns Hopkins for a complete physical exam. With a slight roll of his eyes, he informed me that his wife had arranged the appointment. She wanted him examined by the finest doctors, and Hopkins was the place to find them. Already sensing his answer to my next question, I asked him if they did anything different during their physicals than we do at our office. "No," he said, "it was the same exam. And they couldn't even get the wax out of my ears after several tries. You guys always seem able to get it out, so I made this appointment." After I successfully (and easily) flushed his ears, I told him the doctor at Hopkins must have loosened the wax for me.

As the wave of panic on the sidewalk subsides, I circle around to begin my trek back to the lecture hall. I take notice to the people coming and going from the medical buildings. Some of them are probably patients. Funny how they look just like my patients. And then the obvious dawns on me: at Hopkins, they don't treat alien beings, some higher species that demands only genius-level physicians. People, and their diseases, are the same wherever you go. Granted, some of the best medical minds are at Hopkins and they tackle some of the more difficult medical cases. Yet my place in the medical community is no less important as I intersect with my patients in a meaningful way, helping them along the process of healing.

Slipping into anonymity after graduation to practice medicine in a town few have heard of does not make me any less of a physician. But I'll admit, sometimes I suffer from a career image disturbance. Like a sixteen-year-old girl looking at the digitally perfected bodies on the pages of *Glamour*, I wrestle with how I measure up to famous Christian physicians like Ben Carson and the late Paul Brand—men who accomplished so much and impacted so many in their careers. Or even worse, I compare my career to a medical missionary I know serving in Africa. He has sacrificed so much for the Lord! When I imagine myself standing next to these physicians, my impact seems small; my resume of achievements looks short; my work for God's kingdom feels thin. And instead of being inspired to greater things by these physicians' stories, I focus on my inadequacies and cover my self-perceived flaws with shame.

Yet how quickly I forget the ones who have entrusted their lives to my care. Or the handful of patients who remind me regularly that I saved their lives. Or those that say I am like family to them. Or the ones I have prayed with in a moment of crisis. Or those with whom I have shared the gospel. Or, most importantly, the God who calls me away from these legalistic comparisons and reminds me of the ministry he has handed me in my private practice in a nondescript Pennsylvania suburb.

No matter where you land after residency, no matter what you do in your career, it is all ministry. You don't need to be a famous Christian physician or work at Hopkins or move to the African bush to find your worth as a doctor. God calls you to a great and awesome career—the location and level of acclaim are irrelevant. In fact, God

85

will front-load your career with all the plaudits you need. He speaks the *same* words to you that he spoke to Jesus before the start of his ministry: "This is my Son, whom I love; with him I am well pleased" (Matthew 3:17).

I had no reason to doubt my worth that day in Baltimore; I just needed a reminder of where that worth came from. With confidence restored, I duck back into the lecture hall to finish the day. This is a fine town to visit, but I am needed elsewhere.

Questions for reflection

1. When have you struggled the most with confidence during your medical training?

2. What does this lack of confidence reveal about your heart?

3. How can you place your confidence in what God thinks of you? What could be the results in your career?

Eighteen

Bring the heat

It's as certain as death and taxes, as the saying goes. At some point in your training, probably when you least expect it, someone will yell at you. A jumbo-sized can of emotion will be aimed your way and the red button pushed. Maybe it will be an irate attending blasting you for forgetting to order a lab test, or a cranky, sleep-deprived resident chewing you out for grabbing the wrong size suture, or a patient barking at you for being late to his appointment. It's bound to occur at some point. There's too much pressure, too many fragile egos, and too many sleepless nights in medicine for it never to happen. Maybe you've already had the pleasure.

My most memorable beatdown occurred in my second year of residency. The phone was ringing for me at 8:00 a.m. one Monday morning as I walked into the outpatient clinic. An attending was hunting me down during his rounds at a local nursing home. I picked up the receiver and naively offered some pleasant small talk; the attending responded by going straight for my throat. How dare I treat his patient so poorly, he growled, indulging in an abusive ream-out session for several minutes over how I had managed his nursing home patient while on weekend call. The patient had to be hospitalized, and while he would recover without incident, the family was furious with the attending. He was now ducking and letting their emotion hit me in the face. His words were sharp and personal. He made sure by the time he slammed down the receiver that I questioned my judgement and competence.

As my shaking hand hung up the phone, I stood for several minutes in a tachycardic numbness from the rabid rebuke. My response was at first reflexive; the phone call triggered a flight-or-fight response in me, and if not for the full schedule of patients that morning, I might have quit on the spot and went home. Throughout the morning, the attending's voracious insults echoed in my mind and consumed my self-confidence like a school of piranha.

But there's two sides to that most primal of instincts, and the knot in my stomach was gradually replaced by a strange amalgam of cornered-animal defensiveness and Hugh Glass revenge. As I replayed the weekend events over and over in my mind, a new victim emerged in the story—and the victim was me.

"Why did the attending go ballistic? The patient wasn't harmed, just inconvenienced."

"The nurse who called me that night should have given me a better history about the patient."

"If the attending had taken better care of the patient during the week I wouldn't have been in this mess!"

"The attending is a hot-headed, incompetent fool!"

My anxiety turned to anger, my remorse to resentment. I'm sad to admit, but I began to despise the attending and mocked him in my thoughts, even picking apart his physical flaws. This would become the final version of the events I would tell others: Me—the altruistic, innocent victim of bad teaching, and the Attending—the cold-hearted, volatile, inept aggressor with the bad haircut and funny gait.

I was feeling much better. At least I thought I was.

I don't usually subscribe to the Magic Scripture theory, where you open your Bible to a random passage perfectly suited for the moment, but that's exactly what happened that evening when I got home. I opened to Proverbs 9 and read:

> Whoever corrects a mocker invites insult;
>
> whoever rebukes the wicked incurs abuse.
>
> Do not rebuke mockers or they will hate you;
>
> rebuke the wise and they will love you.
>
> Instruct the wise and they will be wiser still;
>
> teach the righteous and they will add to their learning.
>
> The fear of the Lord is the beginning of wisdom,
>
> and knowledge of the Holy One is understanding.

Much to my dismay, I realized my response to the attending's rebuke did not fit the profile of the wise man. Not even close. And even worse, I could not find any loopholes in this passage. The writer makes no allowances for the harshness of the rebuke. There's no footnote stating that the passage is invalid if cuss words are used or if the person inadvertently spits on you while yelling. Also missing is any excuse for the appropriateness or accuracy of the criticism. Without a doubt, the passage sets its sights not on the rebuke itself, but squarely on the response of the rebukee. I couldn't help but conclude: no matter how strongly the correction is delivered, no matter how misplaced the criticism, no matter how humiliating the experience, my response is what matters most. In fact, the passage suggests my response to the rebuke is a telling indicator of my wisdom (or lack thereof). When my heart burns with the flames of anger and revenge, wisdom calls me to sit in the seat of humility. It beckons me to laser through the smoky clouds of emotion and challenges me to search hard for the lesson found within the message.

With increasing clarity, I realized the patient's hospitalization might have been avoided had I questioned his nurse more carefully. While nurses provide invaluable eyes and ears at the bedside when I am not there, it's my responsibility to ensure I understand what's going on with the patient. Had I not stumbled onto this passage in Proverbs, and had I given into my wounded pride and anger, I would have missed this lesson still valuable today.

It figures, the next day I ran into the attending. For a brief flash, the day-old anger and resentment crept up like stomach juices in my throat. But the words from Proverbs flooded in and neutralized the acidic emotions. It would have been easy to scowl at the attending and resume the mental flogging of him I had so enjoyed the night before. Instead, with God's grace, I chose the narrow path. The smile I greeted him with was genuine and diffused any tension. We stood and talked for a few minutes. I asked about the patient's well-being and complimented the attending on a recent award he had received. As we parted ways, there was a warm glow in my heart. All the anger and resentment had vanished within me, replaced by the Spirit's peace. I had become a wiser man (and a better physician) through it all.

Questions for reflection

1. Recall a time you were yelled at by someone. What feelings did it evoke in you? How did you handle it?

2. How is the fear of the Lord the beginning of wisdom as it says in the Proverbs 9 passage?

3. "Rebuke a wise man and he will love you." How can you become wise like this?

Nineteen

Opportunity doesn't always knock

Did you catch it?

Wait . . . there it is again.

Did you hear it?

You are listening to a patient's history. As the gowned storyteller meanders aimlessly through the history of her present illness, you type choppy sentences on a keyboard. Your mind lines up the next salvo of questions to fire when the patient takes a breath. Clusters of neurons light up as a differential diagnosis forms in your post-call brain.

And then it happens.

But you miss it.

Your mind is too preoccupied with a question: CT or MRI in this case?

And though you are unaware, a piece of the doctor-patient relationship is lost.

What did you miss?

Look for it in this example:

> Doctor: So you are having headaches?
>
> Patient: Yes, I keep getting headaches behind my eyes.
>
> Doctor: I see. When did they start?

Patient: They started about a week ago when one woke me from sleep around 2:00 a.m. My head has never hurt so bad—I thought I was going be sick, you know, throw up. I was really scared because I had heard once that headaches that wake you up could mean you have a tumor or an aneurysm or something. I didn't sleep the rest of that night because my head hurt and I didn't want to fall asleep and not wake up.

Doctor: Did you have any vision changes with the headaches?

Did you catch it? Sure, the doctor asked too many closed-ended questions right off the bat. But more than that, the physician missed . . . an opportunity.

Tucked in amongst the facts of the case (headache of one week's duration, retro-orbital location, nocturnal onset, associated with nausea), there was a hint at something deeper.

A peek behind the curtain.

The patient hinted at emotions stirred by the headaches. ("I was really scared . . . I didn't sleep the rest of that night . . . I didn't want to fall asleep and not wake up.") And therein lies the opportunity. At the moment a patient moves from describing symptoms to revealing emotions behind the symptoms, the physician has a brief but critical opportunity to move from robotic diagnostician to fellow human. It's a short window of time in which to wield one of our greatest tools as physicians—empathy.

Empathy may sound like a fluffy psychological concept that has little place in real world medicine. With all the time constraints doctors face, with all the diagnostic and therapeutic options to wade through, with all the extra baggage loaded into a modern medical visit, who has the time or the energy to be empathetic?

We should. Empathy is what separates us from the car mechanic. Our subjects are not inanimate objects, but ourselves in different skin. To lose empathy is to lose your heart, becoming a mechanical replica of your former self.

And yet empathy shouldn't be hard. All it takes is a quick response: "That sounds painful," or "I would have been scared too," or "A lot of patients tell me they feel the same way." Easy to say, seemingly insignificant, but intrinsically therapeutic for patients. A "kindly word" as William Osler called it, can break through the isolation and loneliness illness creates and provide a needed human "touch" with no epidermal contact.

Perhaps this is an oversimplification. Can a brief phrase spoken to a patient define empathy? Maybe not perfectly. But for a second, the doctor puts herself in the patient's shoes to understand the emotion. It's quick, but done a dozen or so times a day, a warm red glow may return to the physician's chest like E.T. coming back to life.

Why don't patients just come out and say what they're feeling? I have no idea. Maybe it's just human nature to protect that which is most vulnerable and yet most needy in us. Whatever the reason, opportunities for empathy abound in each patient visit and can be as healing as the best broad-spectrum antibiotic that insurance money can buy.

This is not about creating warm fuzzies. Studies suggest practical benefit when empathic opportunities are recognized and addressed by physicians. Patients are more likely to feel heard and understood, improving patient satisfaction; compliance with treatment recommendations increases; office visits tend to be shorter; malpractice suits based on the perception that the physician "just didn't care" may be avoided. In addition, there's direct benefit as well for the physician. Practicing empathy has been shown to prevent burnout, reduce stress, and make medical practice more meaningful.

The hard part is recognizing when these empathic opportunities come along. One study of oncologists videotaped during visits with lung cancer patients found 384 empathic opportunities in twenty visits. Physicians provided an empathic response in only 10 percent of the opportunities.

There may be several reasons for this poor batting average. Physicians may hesitate to acknowledge a patient's feelings, fearing it may launch the visit into a whole new realm, one they don't have time for. Or physicians may feel ill-equipped and poorly trained to address and manage the emotional side of illness, so they avoid it out of feelings of incompetence. Perhaps some physicians feel they *are* caring for patients when they diligently pursue the appropriate diagnosis and treatment. But like a husband who doesn't feel the need to tell his wife he loves her because that's why he goes to work every day, those physicians fail to care for the whole patient (emotions and all) when they miss empathic opportunities.

Christian physicians have a greater calling. Jesus' charge to his disciples in Matthew 10:8 is ours too: "Freely you have received, freely give." God did not diagnose us so we would go and diagnose others; He *loved* us so we would go and do the same. Empathy is that love in action.

Develop the habit of listening for the emotion hidden between the lines of patients' histories. It's there. And do something with it. Don't let yourself be so consumed with obtaining the medical facts that you miss an opportunity to provide empathy to a patient. When

95

you do, both of you will benefit.

Questions for reflection

1. "Freely you have received, freely give." Reflect on how lavishly and unconditionally God has given you his grace, mercy, forgiveness, and blessings. Feel free to write your thought below. Let it soak into your heart and then spill out into your interactions with others.

2. Practice the art of spotting empathic opportunities during patient encounters, or even in your daily conversations with friends or family. Try out a few empathic responses. Watch for the impact. What do you notice?

Twenty

The sheep and the goats: A physician's paraphrase of Matthew 25

When the Great Physician comes in all his glory, and all the angels with him, he will sit on the throne in heavenly glory. All the physicians will be gathered before him, and he will separate them one from another as a shepherd separates the sheep from the goats. He will put the sheep on his right and the goats on his left.

Then the Great Physician will say to those on his right, "Come, you who are blessed by my Father; take your inheritance, the kingdom prepared for you since the creation of the world. For I was depressed and you looked after me with gentleness, I was demanding and you treated me with patience, I was on medical assistance and you showed me respect, I was in chronic pain and you treated me with kindness, I was needy and you showed me compassion, I was alcoholic and you treated me with dignity."

Then the righteous will answer him, "Lord, when did we see you depressed and look after you with gentleness or demanding and treat with you with patience? When did we see you on medical assistance and show you respect, or in chronic pain and treat you with kindness? When did we see you needy or an alcoholic and treat you with dignity?"

Then the Great Physician will reply, "I tell you the truth, whatever you did for one of the least of these brothers of mine, you did for me."

Then he will say to those on his left, "Depart from me, you who are cursed, into the eternal fire prepared for the devil and his angels. For I was depressed and you did not look after me with gentleness, I was demanding and you did not treat me with patience, I was on medical assistance and you did not show me respect, I was in chronic pain and you did not treat me with kindness, I was needy and alcoholic and you did not show me compassion."

They also will answer, "Lord, when did we see you depressed or demanding or on medical assistance or in chronic pain or needy or an alcoholic, and did not help you?"

He will reply, "I tell you the truth, whatever you did not do for one of the least of these, you did not do for me."

Then they will go away to eternal punishment, but the righteous to eternal life.

Questions for reflection

1. How do you respond to this paraphrase?

2. How does this paraphrase compare to the original parable? How would you argue that the parable does not promote salvation by works?

3. I once heard a Pastor remark that one sign of a maturing Christian is a growing concern for the poor and needy. Do you believe this? To what degree is this growing concern present or absent in your life?

4. Which type of patient mentioned in the paraphrase do you struggle with the most? How can you overcome this lack of love?

Twenty-one

In our shoes

Severe abdominal pain . . . a positive pregnancy test . . . an adnexal mass on ultrasound. More than a dry list of symptoms in an obstetrics textbook, these were the realities my wife and I faced on a cloudy June evening in the emergency department. My previous thoughts about ectopic pregnancies were objective, scientific, even distant. But the mental image of my wife undergoing emergent surgery to remove the wayward baby and stop the intraabdominal hemorrhage seared like hot cautery deep within my heart.

Now, as I watch my wife fix her hair in anticipation of being discharged, her frame slightly bent by post-operative pain, I realize these experiences are never wasted on a physician. My compassion and understanding for those with similar experiences has grown beyond measure. Some in academia may cringe at the lack of an evidence-based foundation for this insight. Of course I know better than to base my therapeutic recommendations on one personal event.

But I am a better physician for having to sit alone in the surgical waiting room at midnight, wondering if my wife would be the same person I knew the day before. The treatment protocol for an ectopic pregnancy no longer flashes through my mind as black text from a review article or a monotone voice echoing in a lecture hall; the subject is now full-color and vivid in my mind, enhanced with memories of the metallic smell of blood, the taste of sticky saliva, and the feel of cold, tremulous hands. I have walked where others have walked. Because of this, I am convinced I can care for and connect with them on a deeper level.

Some time ago a seventy-two-year-old Chicago man, in a drunken fog, got his minivan stuck on a railroad crossing as a train barreled toward him. Dan Nugent was sitting in a nearby Starbucks and saw the driver take a wrong turn on the tracks, getting stuck between the crossing gates. Acting quickly and risking his own life, Dan rushed to pull the inebriated driver out of the vehicle moments before the van was crushed by an eastbound train. In an interview later, Dan said, "When I was sitting in Starbucks, it occurred to me that maybe, you know, he had been drinking." What makes this story compelling beyond this simple act of heroism? Turns out Dan Nugent was a recovering alcoholic himself. He told reporters many people had helped him in life and he was happy to help someone else. Can you say, *lifetime supply of Caramel Macchiato*?

Did being a recovering alcoholic help Dan save the driver? Maybe. Perhaps his experience with alcohol enabled him to recognize the driver's actions as inebriated and compelled him to act sooner. But no doubt Dan could empathize with the drunk driver's plight. I'm sure he understood the struggle to ignore the seductive call of alcohol. I bet he remembered the disoriented, spinning feeling from having one too many. And I suspect he didn't judge the driver harshly (like many did online), because he knew how easily it could have been him on those tracks. He had walked where this man had walked; because of this, he was a compassionate savior.

I suppose Jesus could have come to earth a week before Easter, announced he was the Son of God, and died on the cross for our sins. Rigorous theology aside, this saving act would still have qualified as amazing grace. Our salvation still would have been secure. But God's love took it one gigantic step further. Jesus spent thirty-three years as one of us—breathing the same air, dealing with the same annoying people, facing the same temptations—to establish the greatest act of empathy the world has ever known. Jesus walked where we have walked.

In this, a stunning new dimension was added to the act of prayer. Not only was the infinite gap between us and God bridged when Jesus died, giving us access to the throne of grace with confidence, but we also have at the right hand of God a Friend unlike any other, with first-hand knowledge of life here on earth. We can converse freely, not just with the Creator of the Universe (which is mind-blowing in itself), but also with Someone who can say, "I understand what you're going through."

In the surgical waiting room that night, I understood why Jesus came to earth. God could have found a way to save us from afar. He could have provided a savior that died for our sins but was shielded from our dirty lives. But God's relentless love for us would not allow him to do that. His mercy and grace are more than just adequate—they are powerful and creative saving forces that provide more than we could ever ask or imagine. And when we lift our desperate prayers before him, we can know he understands our pain, our loneliness, and our weakness. He has walked where we have walked. He is our Compassionate Savior.

Questions for reflection

1. Have you or a family member experienced medical problems? What impact have they had on your patient care?

2. What have you been dealing with spiritually that you feel God doesn't understand or seem to care about? How does reflecting on the fact that Jesus knows firsthand what you are going through help?

3. Spend time this week reading through the book of John. It shouldn't take you more than an hour or so to read the whole book. Note how Jesus deals with real-life issues, challenges, and temptations. Write your observations here.

Twenty-two

Trainwrecks and survivors

We interrupt this program to bring you a breaking news story...

A news station bursts into the middle of a game show airing after supper. Fidgeting in his seat, the news anchor adjusts his earpiece and struggles to catch up with the teleprompter. Tragedy has struck, he reports somberly. Details are sketchy, but initial reports confirm a commuter train has derailed just outside a major city. The station cuts over to amateur video streaming from the scene. Bouncy pictures show a train lying on its side like a wounded animal. Eviscerated internal contents have spilled out onto the hilly landscape. Box cars litter a wide stretch, scattered in painful angles like dislocated limbs. The camera catches medics shrouding motionless bodies with bleached sheets. Eyewitnesses describe a surreal scene where normalcy was interrupted by the shrill of screeching brakes and the crunch of twisting metal. By the look of things, death and disaster will be tomorrow's headlines.

Train wreck.

Trainwreck is also a term well-seated in the medical vernacular, a slang phrase known universally by healthcare professionals. Trainwreck is the not-so-affectionate nickname given to patients with complicated medical histories, numerous hospital admissions, and a two-page medication list. Computers threaten to crash when a trainwreck's records are retrieved. Just the thought of typing an admission H&P for a trainwreck induces carpal tunnel syndrome. Seeing one's name on an office schedule can ruin the whole day.

The phrase trainwreck is but one of many slang terms the medical profession has adopted, crafted in forms of acronym, abbreviation, colorful image, or downright obscenity. No doubt you are familiar with these sometimes funny but often crude patient labels. Together, they form a secret language, handed down to successive years of students and residents as readily as neurology pearls and surgical techniques.

In their article on medical slang in *Ethics and Behavior*, Fox et al. note:

> slang merely facilitates interrelations among staff, thereby allowing social grouping and rapport. . . . There is little doubt that slang creates a sense of belonging to a select group of individuals and allows surreptitious communication. It also provides humor and witty interaction, which frequently relieves stress. . . . It is also an opportunity for cathartic release from the intensity and hard work of dealing with illness and pain. So, perhaps the discourse is one of physicians working hard, in difficult circumstances, and needing to express and release some of the pressures that accumulate.

Okay, so maybe using slang terms like trainwreck establishes my place among my peers. Maybe the chuckles these labels generate help relieve stress, rescuing hearers ever so briefly from the overwhelming aspects of their jobs. What's the harm, you argue, in using a few colorful terms among coworkers? The old man in the emergency department won't overhear me calling him a Gomer. The mom in the clinic won't be around later when I call her child an FLK. Every doctor has used terms like these during their career—they're as traditional as the Hippocratic Oath. Why make a fuss?

Here's why. What images does the word trainwreck conjure up in your mind? How about violent derailment, dismembered bodies, and torn metal? How about disaster, failure, and death? What would go through the mind of a patient if she overheard me using that phrase to describe her? Think patients don't hear it? Upon yet another one of her hospital admissions, a patient said to me, "I know I'm a trainwreck."

"For the mouth speaks what the heart is full of," Jesus said in Luke 6:45. If this is true, then spouting derogatory and demeaning slang suggests I have a deeper problem than just my vocabulary. In the process of judging, making fun of, or dismissing a patient, I inadvertently crack open my own chest to reveal an increasingly calloused, selfish heart.

Using slang in my everyday conversation, especially with so much of it disparaging to patients, comes at another price too. Fox et al. conclude that, "The use of slang terms may appear to denigrate the patient and therefore lower their consideration in the eyes of the physician." This suggests that each time I use a term like trainwreck, the patient becomes slightly less human in my eyes, eroding a bit of my compassion along the way.

A biblical story is instructive here. The Gospels record numerous encounters Jesus had with the trainwrecks of his time—the lepers, the demon-possessed, the chronically ill. What terms did Jesus use to describe them? His encounter with a sick woman in the Luke 8 reveals his approach—and his heart. Jesus is in the midst of a busy day, surrounded by a large and pressing crowd. Talk about double-booking! In the midst of this chaos he encounters a woman who has been bleeding for twelve years. The bleeding was likely gynecological. Can you imagine this patient showing up in your clinic for a ten-minute appointment?

Never mind the problem of why she has bled for so long—you will also have to address her severe anemia, as well as the profound depression created from years of social isolation (due to this cultural uncleanliness). Mark's version of the story states the woman spent all her money on doctors and instead of getting better, her symptoms worsened. (Luke, a doctor, conveniently left that part out of his version.) As a result, she's probably showing up to her appointment bitter and suspicious of the medical field. So much for staying on time that day.

But look at Jesus' actions. Did he groan about yet another trainwreck to care for? Doubt it. Luke notes Jesus *sought* out the woman from among the crowd and *listened* to her story. He then said to her, "Daughter [a term of endearment at the time], your faith has healed you. Go in peace." Do you sense the tenderness and compassion in his words? Can you feel the hope he instills in those brief sentences? Do you notice the other-centeredness of his approach? Can you catch a glimpse of his heart for one most hurting? This woman left Jesus not just healed physically, but encouraged emotionally and spiritually as well.

Since medical school I have been using a different term instead of trainwreck. I now call these tough patients *survivors*. I figure if slang is part of my daily language at the office and hospital, why not make it positive? I don't need to mortgage my integrity to fit in with my peers; I am smart enough to come up with other ways to mitigate the stress of my profession than by using insults. Survivor is much more patient-centered in its focus than the alternative. Rather than eroding a sense of compassion with each use, a patient-centered term can enhance empathy. And it can be spoken in front of patients without reservation.

Using a word like survivor changes my perspective on several levels. It enables me to focus on a patient's strength, watching another human persevere despite the countless setbacks experienced. I gain a fresh sense of appreciation for the sustaining and healing power of the human body that God has so marvelously created. But just as important, it stirs in me proper empathy for the patient. Every disheartening diagnosis, every hospital admission, every encounter in the patient's gigabyte-consuming electronic chart represents immeasurable pain and suffering. I am navel-gazing when I groan and complain about the patient's multiple medical problems and the inconveniences they cause *me*. How can a few minutes typing an admission H&P or office visit note compare to a lifetime of repeated hospitalizations, shocking cancer diagnoses, painful surgeries, clogged catheters, and infected central lines? My profession may be tough and demanding, but I must remember which side of the scalpel I am on.

"You're a survivor!" I've exclaimed to many patients, and while the results may not be evidence-based, their faces typically brighten at the comment. A patient hearing themselves called a survivor by their doctor may just recover a beat of hope—a hope that may speed healing.

Don't think what you say has that much influence? Listen to what the two wisest men who walked this planet had to say about the subject. One observed, "Reckless words pierce like a sword, but the tongue of the wise brings healing" (Proverbs 12:18). The other said, "For by your words you will be acquitted, and by your words you will be condemned" (Matthew 12:37). There is significant power and sober responsibility in the words we use as physicians—we have the choice whether to use them well.

Questions for reflection

1. Can you remember an episode from your life when someone's words made a lasting impact on you, whether good or bad?

2. How often do you use the word *trainwreck*? Do you think the word warrants abandonment?

3. *"Do not let any unwholesome talk come out of your mouths, but only what is helpful for building others up according to their needs, that it may benefit those who listen." (Ephesians 4:29).*

According to this passage, what two filters should we put our words through before we speak them? What impact would utilizing these two filters have on your conversations?

Twenty-three

The heart of God

Already the morning rages as I walk into the clinic. The daily schedule bursts at the seams. Haphazardly-stacked nursing home communications and FMLA forms threaten an avalanche on my desk. The intercom squawks as staff hunt for me. I take a deep breath, trying to relax the thoracic musculature twisting into knots. Since there is no easy way to enter such a tempest, I submit to the rush and jump in.

When I come up for air, it's already 11:30 am. Time flies when you're overwhelmed. *At least the morning session is almost over,* I mumble under my breath. Then suddenly, like a blow dart to the neck, a new name appears on the computerized schedule, slipped into a noon-time slot that never before existed. Seeing the reason for the visit drains my remaining energy: finger laceration. Guess I have a lunch date.

So many people are coming and going I don't even have a chance to eat. I try to get away by myself to a quiet place and rest— at least for a few minutes. Yet a half-dozen phone calls already wait for me there. When I walk past the waiting room and see the large crowd that awaits, something in me groans.

And then…I think of Jesus.

Mark 6 details a day he had like mine. With a burgeoning ministry, Jesus' schedule fills quickly. Crowds press in around him looking for healing. Dozens, if not hundreds, of voices call out to him in a cacophony of need. On this day, so many people come and go that Jesus and his disciples don't even have a chance to eat. And when they try to slip away for rest and food, the crowd runs ahead to their retreat, waiting like Hollywood paparazzi. Upon seeing the large crowd, Mark reports that Jesus rolled his eyes and complained to the disciples that he would vomit if he had to heal another whining leper.

Okay, you know that's not what happened. That may have been my response, but not his. When Jesus saw the large crowd, "He had compassion on them, because they were like sheep without a shepherd. So he began teaching them many things" (Mark 6:34).

Imagine coming home after an exhausting overnight call and finding a throng of patients waiting for you in your driveway. What would be your response? Duck behind the nearest bushes? Sink down in your car seat and drive past?

Despite being dog-tired and lion-hungry, something stirred in Jesus' heart that roused him into action. Love squelched hunger pangs. Mercy ignored fatigue. Jesus felt deeply for those people, and then acted upon those feelings by giving the "sheep" what they needed: his life-giving words. What fueled this passion of compassion within him? How could he stoke such an internal fire when his day was filled with never-ending demands? Mark gives us the answer: "He had compassion on them, because they were like sheep without a shepherd." Jesus saw the crowd in its overwhelming entirety, but he didn't see them as obstacles to his own agenda or as nameless tools for self-promotion. He viewed them as people lost and wandering, scared and alone, without the One who loved them and could give them provision and identity. Jesus' own needs and desires took a backseat to the love and passion of the Father flowing through him. Jesus' knee-jerk reflex was not to focus on his own needs, but to turn his eyes outward.

In short, Jesus had the heart of God.

It's tempting to think it was easy for Jesus to have God's heart of love and compassion—he had deity coursing through his human veins. Was it really that hard for him? But take one look at his life, how assiduously he cultivated his relationship with the Father. Notice the time he logged on his knees, often before dawn. Observe the God-like character he developed by studying the Father. How did he recall scripture so easily? He memorized it. Jesus may have had the inside track to the throne room of heaven, but he surely didn't abuse the privilege.

If Jesus, the Son of God, devoted so much time and energy to the pursuit of his Father, how much more should I? I can't dive into a pool on the first day of summer and expect to swim like Michael Phelps. Nor can I show up to work, having spent no time with God and expect to be God-like. The rigors of this profession demand I stay in good spiritual shape. Keeping in step with the Spirit in today's medical climate is tough. My grip weakens as I struggle to hold onto compassion and the transcendent purposes of doctoring. The level of erosive forces aligned against me demands I follow Jesus' lead and cultivate my relationship with the One who gives me everything I need for life and godliness (2 Peter 1:3).

This isn't easy. My selfish desires commute with me to work and slip in the door ahead of me. All day they whisper evil nothings in my ear, telling me to satisfy my own needs and ignore those I am called to serve. Too often in the clamor of the day, I obey those voices, like a hypnotized Scooby-Doo. Without God's help I am a hopeless case, a lost sheep myself. Thankfully, I have a patient Savior who is willing to drop everything and search for me when I wander off—which is a daily event. And I pray that in the heat of the day, my response to the overwhelming flood of need around me will be with a heart that beats like Jesus' that in turn beats like God's.

Questions for reflection

1. Where have you seen the overwhelming aspects of medicine sap the compassion in your life?

2. How well do you stay in good spiritual shape to handle the demands of people you encounter?

3. What can you do this week to follow Jesus' example of cultivating a relationship with the Father?

Twenty-four

A mountain of debt

Cleaning out my home office the other day, I stumbled upon the promissory notes I signed before starting medical school. How bold and naively confident my signature looks on every line, with each goldenrod page committing me to tens of thousands of dollars in student loan debt. At the time, I should have been horrified at the amount of debt a person could accumulate in fifteen minutes. But I don't recall giving it a second thought as I sat in that loan office many years ago. I had bigger things to worry about that day—Gross Anatomy would be starting soon. Besides, wouldn't I make boatloads of cash in my future career and pay off those loans in a year or two?

Medical students today have it much worse. My loan amounts would probably only buy a first-year student her textbooks! The point is, no matter how many zeros and commas we have in our student loan account balances, we in medicine are well accustomed to debt. Our careers begin deep in the red, and I'm not talking blood. But that's why a verse in Romans can resonate on such a familiar level with professional borrowers like us.

> Let no debt remain outstanding except the *continuing debt* to love one another, for whoever loves others has fulfilled the law.
>
> Romans 13:8, italics mine

I will owe Sallie Mae a hefty payment every month for years into the future. But even more impressive is the huge tab I have run up with God for my salvation. I know that full well. Through his amazing grace he has saved me and given me new life, hope, and purpose. I can't love and praise him enough for what he has done for me. But am I in debt to *other people,* as Paul suggests in the verse above? Sure, I owe my parents for bringing me into this world, and I owe my wife big time for putting up with me every day. I still have a fifteen-year mortgage as well. And I should return *La La Land* to Redbox before I owe a fortune on it. But I can't imagine I am in debt to many other people. So what's Paul getting at?

To understand Paul's point, the verse above needs context. Chapter 13 sits deep in the pragmatic section of the book of Romans. True to form, Romans is divided up like most of Paul's books into an initial *Why* section, followed by the *Now what* of practical application. Heralded by the "Therefore" at the start of Chapter 8, Paul goes on to describe how we are to live in response to the once-for-all, life-bringing, perfect act of justification in the sacrifice of Jesus he argued for in the first seven chapters.

So when Paul writes of a continuing debt I have to love others in the passage above, he seems to suggest that I am indebted to others *because* of what Jesus did for me. Jesus took my sin on himself when he went to the cross—a gift of love from the Father—and thus I owe him my life. But in a stunning turn of events, God says, "To show me love for what I have done for you, love other people." It's the ultimate Pay-It-Forward plan.

In a way, while God knows I could never repay the debt I owe him, he wants me to try. And every day God sends people into my life looking for a return on his investment. One of those people triggers my beeper in the middle of the night. One cuts me off on the way to work. One needs a price check in the grocery store line in front of me. One shows up twenty minutes late for his appointment and expects to be seen.

I can try to love these people out of a sense of obligation to God, which is not necessarily wrong. Obligation can bring a sober discipline to love, and it comes through even when the warm fuzzies of love and compassion are absent. But loving out of obligation is like using the trial version of a software program—the features are limited. Obligatory love doesn't go beyond basic minimal requirements. And ultimately, it can feel like a ball and chain I cannot shake.

So how should I view this continuing debt to love others? At least one person Jesus met knew the answer. While reclining at a Pharisee's table in Luke 7, Jesus received a conversation-interrupting footbath from a prostitute using a concoction of perfume, tears, and hair to clean the dirt off his toes. It was a daring display of honor and humility from someone who had no business hanging around Pharisees and Rabbis, the "1%" of the day. The dinner host was shocked, aghast that Jesus would allow a "sinner" to touch him. But it's the prostitute, not the scripture-expert Pharisee who would have understood Paul's point. Jesus reveals the motivation behind the woman's outpouring of love: she loved much because she had been forgiven much. The woman's tears flowed from a clear understanding of the magnitude of mercy she had been given. Her overwhelming debt paid for by overwhelming forgiveness fueled an overwhelming gratefulness in her to the point she was willing to risk it all (a prostitute in a Pharisee's house uninvited!) to pour out her love and gratitude.

I need help remembering the debt I owe God—that inexhaustible, insurmountable, immoveable mountain I will never be able to repay. Even if I lived every day like Mother Teresa, I wouldn't make the tiniest of dents in the sum I owe my Savior. But that's the point: my debt to God is so overwhelmingly huge, it should make me overwhelmingly grateful and compel me to pour out love on those God puts in my path each day.

Every month e-mails arrive, reminding me of the student loans I still owe. The day they will stop coming seems too far off to be possible. So for now, I have a continuing debt. The same is true of my debt to those I encounter each day, thanks to the amazing grace shown to me. I will never be able repay the debt I owe. But each day, with extreme gratitude, I should try.

Questions for reflection

1. How do you practice remembering what God has done for you? How might you foster this?

2. If you're honest with yourself, how do you view others? With a sense of entitlement, believing they owe you? Seeing them as obstacles to step over to achieve your daily goals? Or with a grateful indebtedness to them?

3. How might your life look different if you lived with a continuing debt perspective?

4. Who is one person you can love better today to show gratitude to God?

Twenty-five

Seeing stars

This is a perfect ending to a perfect day, I thought to myself as I lay in the middle of my apartment complex parking lot. It was after midnight on a cold January night, and I had just finished another twelve-hour shift early in my residency. The night had been one that makes you question whether you chose the right profession. My clinical acumen was off all night. Tests I had ordered, expecting them to confirm my diagnoses, were negative. I was slow and inefficient. The attendings pimped me on information I didn't know. I neglected to order a test on a patient that delayed his discharge for hours. My bedside manner was atrocious. Fortunately, my disastrous night harmed no patients—my only success. The twelve-hour shift felt like a year.

When I left, two hours late, I was beaten, bruised, and bitter. *What was I doing in this profession anyway? I'm sure the attending thought I was a loser. How am I going to be a good doctor? Had I learned anything about medicine in the past five years?* I thought of my non-medical friends, at home and asleep (debt free) in their beds—*was I crazy for choosing this career?*

The questions continued to hound me as I pulled into the parking lot and stepped out of my car. So much doubt and disillusionment clouded my vision I failed to notice the patch of ice on the way to the door. Down I went, sprawled out like Marv in one of his many wipeouts from the movie *Home Alone*. The spill jolted me so unexpectedly that it knocked the swirling questions out of my head. Suddenly everything was quiet—and still.

After concluding I was not unconscious, I realized my new position afforded me a perfect view of a clear night sky. A full complement of stars studded the darkness, the new moon deferring to the celestial cast that night. The air was still, the apartment complex hushed, and my sky view unobstructed save for the momentary haze from my exhalations. It had been a long time since I had stopped to look at the cosmos—and a long time since I had been this quiet.

In that moment I realized why the Psalmist wrote, "Be still and know that I am God" (Psalm 46:10). For as I lay on the cold pavement looking at the expanse above, my life seemed tiny. Yet God felt very near. Like he was laying in the parking lot next to me. And I felt him saying, "Do you see these stars? I created each one, hand picking its position in the evening sky. The Little Dipper was *my* idea. There are millions of other stars you cannot see that I hold in place. If I can handle these gigantic balls of superheated gases, don't you think I am capable of guiding your little life? I will make you into a good physician. Trust me, I know something about healing people. I will ensure you learn what you need to know. But you need to find your worth in what I think of you, not in others' opinions, not in your performance, and certainly not in your medical knowledge. I've got a saying that may help you, which I know you've heard before: Trust in me with all your heart and lean not on your own understanding."

Untangling our identities from our medical careers is painfully arduous. Many of my friends, when asked what they do for a living, say, "I work at So-and-So Company" or "I'm in sales." When asked, I say, "I *am* a doctor." Being a physician is not just my nine-to-five job. It defines me. People call me "Doc" at church, in the grocery store, on the golf course. Family and friends ask for medical advice anytime I'm around. A substantial proportion of my identity is wrapped up in my profession. My hands grip tightly to the diploma I worked so hard (and paid so much) to obtain. But God demands the entirety of my identity be turned over to him. He demands complete trust. He wants all of my heart. He will not settle for part.

Why not? Why won't God give us a break and let us squirrel away part of our identity for ourselves? Why is he so ruthless in his pursuit of total surrender? Because he knows us. He knows if we keep possession of even the smallest morsel of our lives, we will turn it into the Ultimate Thing and worship it. God loves us too much and has invested too much (a.k.a. his son Jesus) to let that happen. His way is the Path of Life. It is only in surrender of your complete identity to God that you will find your true identity and find true freedom to practice medicine the way he created you to.

At the end of my life, I want to look back and see that I used my medical career, not as the foundation of my identity and confidence, but rather as a well-worn trowel to help build God's kingdom. In the end, I want to hand God my medical school diploma, tell him thanks for letting me borrow it, and hear him say, "Well done, good and faithful servant."

When I finally stood up that January night, I was glad nothing hurt. I did not want to go back to the hospital too soon.

Questions for reflection

1. Was there a time you questioned whether you belonged in medicine? What triggered the doubt? Was it a mistake you made? A poor score on an exam? What does this reveal about where you place your confidence and competence as a physician?

2. Where do you go to be still and know God? When was the last time you were there? How can you work regular time in God's presence into your schedule?

3. What do you want to see when you look back at the end of your career?

Afterword

I reference quotes from a number of important books, several of which are classics of the Christian faith. Three of my favorites are listed below. I encourage you to read them. Each has had a critical role in growing my faith, starting in college and extending through my medical school and residency years.

The Pursuit of God, by A.W. Tozer

The Ragamuffin Gospel, by Brennan Manning

The Practice of the Presence of God, by Brother Lawrence

Acknowledgements

Thanks to Donna Conley, Nancy Mehesy, and Jordan Blackbird for reviewing all or part of this book. Their feedback and insights were invaluable.

This book was self-published using Createspace. The cover was crafted using Canva and formatted with Gimp.

Cover photos by Leung Cho Pan and Dutourdumonde Photography.

References

Chapter 1: Comparisons

Brennan Manning, *The Ragamuffin Gospel: Good News for the Bedraggled, Beat-Up, and Burnt Out* (Sisters, OR: Multnomah Books, 1990)

Jennifer Kennedy Dean, *He Restores My Soul: A Forty-Day Journey Toward Personal Growth* (Nashville, TN: B&H Publishing Group, 1999), pg 83.

Chapter 3: The thrill of victory

Eugene Peterson, *A Long Obedience in the Same Direction: Discipleship in an Instant Society.* (Downers Grove, Illinois: InterVarsity Press,1980), p.96.

Chapter 4: It's who you know

Francis Shaeffer, *The Mark of a Christian* (Downers Grove, Illinois: InterVarsity Press, 1970), p. 9.

Chapter 5: Moments around the fire

A.W. Tozer, *Man: The Dwelling Place of God* (Camp Hill, Pennsylvania: Christian Publications, 1966), p.160.

Chapter 7: Pride comes before...

AW Tozer, *The Pursuit of God* (Camp Hill, Pennsylvania: Christian Publications, 1982), p. 166.

Chapter 8: Right here

Simons, Daniel J and Chabris, Christopher F. "Gorillas in our midst: sustained inattentional blindness for dynamic events", Perception, 1999, volume 28, pages 1059-1074.

Chapter 10: A headful

AW Tozer, *That Incredible Christian*. Compiled by Anita M. Bailey (Camp Hill, Pennsylvania: Christian Publications, 1964), p.92.

Timothy Keller with Kathy Keller, *The Songs of Jesus* (New York: Viking, 2016), p. 304.

Chapter 11: The monk and the four-eyed fish

AW Tozer, *The Pursuit of God* (Camp Hill, Pennsylvania: Christian Publications, 1982), p. 127.

Information about and quotes by Brother Lawrence from:
Brother Lawrence, *The Practice of the Presence of God with Spiritual Maxims* (Grand Rapids, MI: Baker Publishing Group, 22nd printing, 2007).

Robert Elmer, *Practicing God's Presence: Brother Lawrence for Today's Reader* (Colorado Springs, CO, 2005).

Chapter 15: Temple dwelling

AW Tozer, *The Pursuit of God* (Camp Hill, Pennsylvania: Christian Publications, 1982), p. 127.

Lola Ogunnaike, "Fan's Therapy: 'Today' and Yesterdays", *New York Times*, May 31,2006,
http://www.nytimes.com/2006/05/31/arts/television/31lenn.html.

Rick Schindler, "Sad news: TODAY superfan Linny Boyette has passed away", *Today*, October 7, 2013. http://www.today.com/allday/sad-news-today-superfan-linny-boyette-has-passed-away-8C11339494.

"Rollen Stewart," *Wikipedia*. Last modified February 9, 2017
http://en.wikipedia.org/wiki/Rollen_Stewart.

Sinclair Ferguson, *A Heart for God* (Colorado Springs, Colorado: Navpress,1985), p. 150.

Chapter 16: The least of these

Loxterkamp, David MD. "Facing Our Morality: The Virtues of a Common Life", JAMA. Vol. 282, p. 923: Sept. 8, 1999.

Chapter 19: Opportunity doesn't always knock

Morse DS, Edwardsen EA, Gordon HS. Missed opportunities for interval empathy in lung cancer communication. *Arch Intern Med*, 2009; 168(17): 1853-1858.

Suchman AL, Markakis K, Beckman HB, Frankel R. A model of empathic communication in the medical interview. *JAMA*. 1997; 277(8): 678-682.

Chapter 21: In our shoes

Information on the seventy-two-year-old Chicago man from:

"Good Samaritan pulls man from train tracks minutes before fiery collision," accessed online at www3.whdh.com/news/articles/national/BO72141, January 31, 2008.

"Seconds from Death," accessed online at www.foxnews.com/story/0,2933,327068,00.html, July 22, 2009.

Chapter 22: Trainwrecks and survivors

Fox, AT, Fertleman M, Cahill P, Palmer RD. *Medical slang in British hospitals*, Ethics & Behavior, 2003. *13*(2), 173–189.

Made in the USA
Lexington, KY
28 November 2017